Praise f

"Dr. Paul has developed a comprehensive, integrative, and holistic approach to Sleep. This book is filled with safe, effective, science-based strategies that will promote sleep without requiring addictive medications. Patients struggling with sleep and clinicians treating sleep problems will find the solutions given in Sleep Coaching immensely beneficial."

James Greenblatt, MD
Chief Medical Officer, Walden Behavioral Care
Author of Finally Focused, Breakthrough Depression Solution

"The importance of sleep for health and vitality has long been recognized although practical advice has been sketchy. This book is packed with tips and strategies for improving sleep based on research, presented in a manner that the layperson and the nonmedical counselor can efficiently use. It is a valuable contribution to the field and well worth including in a personal library of wellness strategies."

Barry Hensel, PhD
Vice President, Circles of Care, Florida

"Dr. Paul has written the perfect manual for sleep coaching. Sleep Coaching is the best book available which will teach effective natural ways to fall asleep without sleeping pills. Follow this book and have a sound sleep each night & every night."

Adolf Casal, MD
Medical Director, Children's Healthcare of Atlanta
& Atlanta center of Eating Disorder

"An outstanding book which offers groundbreaking sleep strategies. Dr. Paul has written a passionate and practical guide for the often overlooked, but the most crucial aspects of healthy living. Read Sleep Coaching to harness the rejuvenating and restorative power of sleep."

Roy Sanders, MD
Fellow of American Psychiatric Association
Author, How to Talk to Parents About Autism

"Lack of sleep can be a risk factor for various ailments including cancer. Sleep Coaching offers a powerful and effective alternative solution to sleep problems afflicting millions of Americans. It is one of the best books on lifestyle-based cognitive, behavioral and environmental approaches to get deep restorative sleep. Sleep Coaching is a must read for all who want to live a long healthy life."

Abhimanyu Ghose, MD, FACP
Cancer Specialist, Arizona Oncology

"As an interventional cardiologist, I have seen how vital sleep is for your heart. Sleep Coaching is a remarkable book! Dr. Paul has penned the perfect book for all sleep problems. This comprehensive guide will coach you to sleep naturally without meds. This book is undoubtedly the type of work that in my opinion provides direct benefits to the medical field and other medical subspecialties in our country and to the patients that we treat."

Ankush Moza, MD
Interventional Cardiologist,
Hurley Medical Center, Flint, Michigan

Praise for Sleep Coaching- Cont.

"As a cardiovascular and diabetes researcher, I can say that sleep problems increase the propensity for high blood pressure, high cholesterol, and diabetes. Most of the findings confirming these spans over numerous medical journals and often confusing. Dr. Paul has done a brilliant job in condensing the complex research findings in simple, straightforward guidelines that everyone can follow. This book lays down all the natural ways of getting sleep without becoming dependent on sleeping pills. This information is immensely valuable because practicing the right methods of sleeping decreases the risks of heart attack, stroke, and cancer."

Sumit Monu, PhD
Research Scientist at the Hypertension and Vascular Research Division,
Henry Ford Hospital in Detroit, Michigan

"In this informative and well-written volume, Dr. Paul has given a powerful non-drug treatment for insomnia. Sleep coaching is a significant addition to the medical sciences which offers safe, effective, proven non-drug remedies for sleep. At a time when millions are dying from the prescription drug overdoses, the natural sleep cures provided in this book can save millions of lives."

Vipul Khetarpaul, MD
Vascular Surgeon,
The Iowa Clinic-West Des Moines Campus

"A landmark book on the nature of sleep, insomnia, and natural sleep remedies. One of the best book on mind-body health which covers all aspects of sleep. We sleep a third of our lives, and its secrets are a mystery for most. Not anymore. Dr.Paul shows the most effective sleeping pills are within us, and we can harness the power of sleep by using our own body's inbuilt sleep drive. A significant contribution not only to the field of neurosciences, but all medical specialties as sleep can heal or harm all organ systems."

Ankur Agarwal, MD
Obstretician-Gynecologist, Chillicothe, Missouri

"As a researcher in neuroscience imaging, I can say that sleep deprivation can impair all aspects of the brain function. Dr. Paul's book provides practical tips about insomnia, sleep apnea, child sleep, and night work. Sleep coaching will guide you on the use of mindfulness, meditation, diet, exercise, and stress management as a way to get deep restorative sleep. A must read for all."

Suprateek Kundu, PhD
Assistant Professor at Department of Biostatistics,
Emory University, Atlanta Georgia

"As a child specialist, I can say that sleep plays a crucial role in the growth and development of babies. Dr. Paul has masterfully explained the developmental and evolutionary needs of a newborn. The book provides ideal sleep solutions for all ages."

Anjali B Nayak, MD
University Oklahoma Health Science Pediatric Nephrology
Oklahoma City, Oklahoma

Sleep Coaching

Easy Sleep Without Meds

Science-Based Cognitive, Behavioral, Environmental, & Integrative Sleep Solutions

Panchajanya 'Panch' Paul, MD

ISBN-13: 978-1725075948
ISBN-10: 1725075946

Cover Picture Niraj Sharma

Cover Model Sagnika Mukherjee

Cover Design Zeeshan Abid (Znamide @Fiverr)

Author Picture by John Gladson

Interior Formatting by www.fiverr.com/mehrangull

Dedicated to My Parents

Pratul Paul

&

Kshama Paul

Contents

Forward

Dr. Paul has written a concise but thorough analysis of sleep as it applies to all individuals-those with and without mental illness. He takes an understandably practical approach as he begins with the history and anthropological implications of the importance of sleep in human development working his way towards practical solutions to overcome sleep disorders and improve one's daily functioning.

Dr. Paul's incorporation of exercise, nutrition, mindfulness, and stress management techniques is essential for good sleep and the maintenance of proper health for all adequately functioning persons.

Sleep Coaching is undoubtedly one of the best and the most practical book which teaches cognitive, behavioral, and environment modifications based on scientific evidence to promote sleep. In my opinion, this book will prove valuable both to the layperson and to the mental health practitioner seeking easy to implement sleep solutions.

It should be required reading for all students entering the medical field, and even for those who have spent many years in the field of sleep disorders. Psychiatry has long been awaiting a practical manual to assist those unduly affected by sleep problems. Dr. Paul had certainly delivered on this need and his promise to educate.

Todd M. Antin MD, DFAPA
CEO, PACT ATLANTA LLC

Distinguished Fellow of American Psychiatric Association
Board Certified in Adult, Addiction, Geriatric, and Forensic Psychiatry
Atlanta's Top Psychiatrist,1999-2018, by Atlanta Magazine

WHY SLEEP COACHING?

I have worked as a psychiatrist and have provided mental health treatment to children, adolescents, and adults. During my clinical practice, I have encountered many people suffering from sleep problems. Most of the psychiatric disorders like Major Depressive Disorder, Generalized Anxiety Disorder, Bipolar Disorder and Posttraumatic Disorder comes with sleep disturbance. Some of them are easily treatable and some not so. Many times, it is easier to treat the core psychiatric problems as compared to the sleep issues.

As the name suggests, this book is about sleep coaching. A coach is someone one who instructs and trains. The primary focus of this book is to coach easy ways to promote sleep. People may wonder and question, since so much information is freely available on the internet, why another book?

The internet is full of information and advice; many of them are useful. However, there are technical details with ambiguities and contradictory opinions. It is sometimes difficult for people to fathom all intricacies without medical training. Even medical professionals disagree on specific topics. In this book, I have simplified all the relevant research findings and recommendations in a clear, coherent narrative.

Although sleep problems have inflicted civilized people for hundreds of years, research on sleep medicine is relatively new. There is yet to be a sleep medication to be discovered, which can be taken for a long term without adverse effects. Research shows that taking the conventional sleeping pills, in the long run, poses serious health hazards. Don't get me wrong. Sleeping pills can be lifesaving when used prudently, but their long-term safety is questionable. As every physician has to take the Hippocratic oath and abide by the "primum-non-nocere" (first do no harm) doctrine; I began my search for SAFE sleep solutions.

Since sleep science is new, many physicians are not yet aware of the dangers of sleep deprivations. Physicians themselves are one of the most sleep-deprived members of the society. Thus in-spite of having many solutions available for sleep-related problems, many patients are struggling with their sleep and are forced to take sleeping pills, which is not healthy in the long term. This has prompted many physicians like me to seek safer sleep solutions for our patients.

If you are among the millions of Americans who struggle with sleep each night and are tired because of lack of sleep — this book is for you. If you want to improve sleep to maximize your productivity, creativity, and the efficiency-this book is for you. Also, if you are someone who has to travel across multiple time zones; or if you are a shift worker with irregular work hours- then this book will guide you to get better sleep.

The book will also coach you to harness the power of sleep to get more energy, lose extra weight, look younger feel happier, and fight better against diseases.

Lastly, this book can help internists, psychiatrists, psychologists, nurses, nurse practitioners, social workers-

anyone and everyone who is there to help people with sleep sufferings. Clinicians will find many useful practical tools to coach their clients and solve sleep problems.

Panchajanya Paul, MD

August 15, 2018

Introduction

In this fast 24x7 globalized society, sleep is the last activity scheduled for the day. It becomes the calamity whenever any change of plan occurs. One may lose sleep when one is fired (due to stress), or when one is hired (excessive celebration), and even when promoted (excessive work). Unless one is careful and cognizant, the loss of sleep can accumulate over time leading to sleep debt, and our body began to go through the adverse effects of sleep deprivation.

Half of my patients come with sleep problems. As many of us spend most of our time indoors perusing sedentary jobs- sleep problems are on the rise across the globe. Sleep can mimic, trigger, and exacerbate all psychiatric conditions.

Inadequate sleep will cause poor attention and focus the next day mimicking Attention deficit hyperactivity disorder (ADHD). Lack of sleep will cause low mood, lethargy, irritability mimicking depression. Sleep deprivation for consecutive days may trigger life-threatening psychotic or a manic episode. Moreover, the good news is- Restful sleep will promote the brain healing and alleviate the symptoms of depression, anxiety, bipolar, ADHD and psychosis.

I am a board-certified child, adolescent, and adult psychiatrist. I also practice integrative and holistic medicine. From my clinical practice and research, I am convinced that sleep is vital for health and well-being. I will discuss here: how in various ways sleep is essential to us and what we can do to get better quantity and quality sleep. I have seen numerous people suffer from sleep problems along with their mental and physical health challenges.

Sleep is a vital element of our survival. We spend nearly one-third of our lives in sleep, yet there is a lack of awareness about this topic among people and surprisingly many health care providers. I will address here all the things I wish I could say to all my patients and all those people who are suffering because of lack of understanding of the sleep processes. Also, it is more convincing to describe things in a written material using various quotes and references from other leading experts.

Unfortunately treating insomnia is not easy. All conventional prescription sleep medications come with adverse effects if used in the long run.

Commonly prescribed medicines like Valium and Xanax are highly addictive and increases the risk of memory loss and dementia. Other sleep medications like Ambien, Lunesta are reported to cause sleepwalking, behavioral changes, and cognitive problems. Off-label medicines for sleep like Seroquel and Remeron increases body weight, blood cholesterol, and blood pressure. Antihistamine medications like Vistaril and Benadryl have less severe side effects, but patients can develop tolerance requiring even higher doses with time. Same is true with tricyclics like Trazodone and Doxepin.

While the search for a magic sleep pill goes on, we can all sleep better by following natural ways to facilitate the body's natural sleep drive. This book will coach you on the effective natural ways to boost sleep.

Sleep Science is a new, young and exciting branch of medicine. We still don't know — why we sleep? Why we dream? Moreover, many other mysteries of sleep remain elusive. However, there is good news. Although late to start with, sleep has now captured the interest of many scientists and researchers. We have information on what happens during sleep in our brain and body. We also know what happens when we don't get enough sleep. Based on these, we have evidence-based interventions to help us with sleep.

Science progresses when experts in the field have researched, analyzed and verified the theories and reached a consensus. Sleep research is a new branch and one of the youngest in medicine. There remain many areas in sleep research where the expert consensus has not yet been reached. I have taken the liberty to assume that the primary goal of the readers for this book is to sleep better each night and every night.

I have included some relevant research to explain the science behind the recommendations. Knowing the rationale will empower the readers to tweak the advice for their condition. Wherever there are ambiguity and disagreement among experts, I have chosen the explanation which appears most logical to me and agrees with my personal and professional experience.

This book is written for the layperson in mind. I have tried to write in an easy, straightforward manner so that people without a medical or scientific background can understand. I have limited the use of jargons except when necessary. Enthusiastic readers seeking more knowledge can refer to the sources and suggested readings at the end of the book. Many chapters of the book were published in health magazines as independent articles.

Each chapter can stand on its own. Readers can read from beginning to end or start with any chapter of their interest and proceed forward. The only drawback may be some repetitions of the essential themes, which I think may further reinforce healthy sleeping habits.

PART I
NORMAL SLEEP

Chapter 1

WHAT IS SLEEP?

Life can be divided into two states: Sleep and Wake. Some consider dreaming as the third phase, but for scientific purposes, dreaming is considered to be a part of sleep. Sleep is a period of rest for the body and the mind, during which voluntary control is lost, and the conscious bodily functions are suspended. During sleep, we are immobile with low sensitivity to external stimuli.

We spend more than one-third of our lives in sleep. No one knows exactly why? Sleep has been shrouded with mysteries, myth, and dread since early times. Greeks thought sleep and death to be intertwined, and the joint product of night and darkness. Thus, the birth of Hypnos (the god of sleep) and his twin brother Thanatos (God of death) from the union of mother Nyx (God of the night) and father Erebos (God of darkness).

However, ancients acknowledged sleep essential to survival and attributed mystical properties to it. Sleep always played a fundamental role in the healing rituals of the ancient and medieval world.

The Renaissance heralded the age of discoveries culminating in the industrial revolution. The invention of electric light by Edison paved the way for 24x7 work and productivity. Modern commerce demanded more work and less leisure, and the value of sleep was de-emphasized. It was thought to be a state of passivity and inactivity. Many intellectuals,

Edison prominent among them, began to question the value of sleep. Edison claimed to have slept only 4 hours per night and encouraged others to do so. It was even debated if sleep is essential at all, or how can it be eliminated to herald a 24x7 period of work and leisure.

Part of this confusion was due to the limited understanding of sleep. There were two problems in studying sleep. Firstly, sleep originates in the brain. The brain is boxed inside the rigid skull and studying its action from outside without causing damage is difficult. Secondly, we never know we are in sleep when we are asleep. All we can recall are a few dreams, without any active, experiential knowledge of sleep. Because of these limitations, the science of sleep remained in darkness till the beginning of the 20th century.

The scientific investigation on sleep lagged those of other processes like eating (digestion), breathing (respiration) and blood circulation. Many thought that the brain might have electrical activity, but there was no way to know or prove that. The breakthrough came in 1924 when German physiologist and psychiatrist recorded the first human brain electrical activity and plotted them on a piece of paper. Berger developed the machine and called it electroencephalogram. The discovery of EEG is considered pivotal in neurosciences. Berger missed the Nobel prizes because of the world war II and his untimely death in 1941.

But the science of sleep lunged forward by leaps and bounds. With the EEG, the hitherto dark world of sleep became alive and active. EEG was soon adopted across research labs all over Europe and USA. Rapid progress was made in sleep neurophysiology.

Sleep can be divided into two stages as per the electrical activity recorded through the EEG. When we observe someone sleeping, many times, we notice that his or her eyes albeit closed, are moving rapidly. This stage is the rapid eye movement sleep (REM), which shows high electrical activity in the EEG and is associated with dreams. However, during most of our sleep, the eyes do not move, and this phase is called the Non-Rapid Eye Movement Sleep (NREM).

When we close our eyes and slowly drift to sleep, we enter the stages of NREM sleep. NREM sleep has three stages. The first two stages (N1, N2) are the light sleep that we experience in the beginning. Our senses remain partially active, and one can be easily aroused from this stage. The third stage of NREM (N3) is composed of slow waves. The brain reaches a stage of quiescence with slowing down of all the brain waves. This deepest stage of NREM is also called slow wave sleep, and the term NREM and slow wave sleep are sometimes used interchangeably. The slow wave sleep is essential for survival, and it is the period when the body does the major repair work, and growth happens.

After the light and deep stages of sleep, we enter the dream stage of sleep also known as the REM. During this time, there is rapid eye movements seen, hence the name Rapid Eye Movement Sleep.

The brain is firing rapidly during the REM stage with all fast waves as if we are still awake. The brain electrical activity of a person in REM sleep is indistinguishable from a waking person. The cause for the high brain activity during dream stage of sleep remains a mystery.

The discovery of REM was made accidentally by Nathaniel Kleitman's and his student Eugene Aserinsky. They also linked the rapid eye movements with the vivid dreams that happen during sleep. William C Dement working at Kleitman's sleep lab at that time, confirmed this by awakening volunteers during the REM sleep, and everyone could recall his or her dreams.

Other peculiar features of REM are the tendency for rapid eye rolling movement and complete loss of all muscle tone. It has been hypothesized that the loss of muscle tone during REM is a protective mechanism to prevent us from acting out our dreams.

The muscle paralysis during dream sleep was confirmed in an experiment by researcher Michael Jouvet. He made lesions around the brain of cats which blocked the muscle paralysis associated with REM sleep. This cats thus retained muscle activity even during the REM sleep. The cats were found to do bizarre movement during sleep, like raising their paws to grab some imaginary mice, jumping to catch an imaginary bird, and other complex movements as if the cats were dreaming attacks, defense, and exploration.

Chapter 2

WHAT IS SLEEP ARCHITECTURE?

So far, we learned that when we sleep the electrical activity of our brain changes repeatedly. Based on brain electrical activity, sleep is broadly divided into two types: NREM and REM sleep. NREM is further classified into light and deep sleep. Sleep architecture refers to this structural organization of sleep into various sleep types through which body cycles through the night. Now let us study how sleep is organized throughout the night amongst its multiple stages.

Each sleep cycle and lasts about 90 minutes. The proportion of NREM and REM changes through the night. Each night people experience between 4 to 6 sleep cycles. Sleep follows a predictable pattern and moves back and forth between the three stages: NREM (Light and Deep sleep), and REM sleep.

The percentage of deep sleep (slow wave sleep) remains high during the first half of the night and gradually declines in the latter half. On the other hand, REM sleep percentage increase with each subsequent cycle peaking in the last periods. The first REM sleep cycle lasts only about 10 minutes and the last one lasts about an hour. Thus, the longer you sleep, the more likely you are to have dreams. I have seen many sleep-deprived patients cannot recall any dreams. Many say that they don't dream at all.

The sequence of a Sleep Cycle

NREM: Light Sleep (40-55 percent total sleep time in adults)	The light sleep is the first stage of sleep. It is the time of transition from awakening to sleep. People have easy arousal from this state. The heart rate and body temperature drop preparing the body for deeper sleep.
NREM: Deep Sleep (15-25 percent total sleep time in adults)	This is the deepest state of sleep. All the blood flow is transferred from the brain to the muscles. The brain becomes quiet and shows slow waves on EEG. It's most difficult to awake from this deepest state of sleep.
REM: Dream Sleep (20-25 percent total sleep time in adults)	The brain becomes active, have fast waves, the eye moves rapidly, dreaming occurs. Heart rate and blood pressure increases. Arm and leg muscles remain paralyzed.

The stages of sleep follow a sequential pattern when we go to sleep: light to deep to REM/Dream to light to deep. However, we can be awake at any stage of sleep. People going to bed at night tends to get up in the morning which marks the end phase of our sleep cycle. During that time people are mostly in light sleep or REM sleep. It is relatively more comfortable to get up from those stages.

Getting up from a light sleep stage is more desirable. When we get up from the REM sleep, we remember the dreams. Getting up from a deep sleep (slow wave sleep) state is most difficult and results in sleep-inertia. Sleep inertia is a condition when we feel groggy and disoriented after getting up and need about 20-30 minutes to get back our full cognitive capability.

The sleep architecture changes as we age. The percentage of REM sleep decreases with time. REM sleep dominates the unborn fetus occupying 80% of the time. At birth, a newborn has 50 percent or more of their sleep in REM. With time the REM sleep decrease and the NREM sleep increases.

At four months' newborn has 40 percent REM and 60 percent NREM sleep. By early adulthood, this number stabilizes to around 25 % REM and 75 % NREM which remains stable till old age. REM or dream sleep is associated with learning new information. The younger you are, the more REM sleep you have, the more is your ability to learn new things. Babies have the maximum REM sleep, because they are soaking every information around them like a sponge.

Age	REM %	NREM %
Unborn fetus	80	20
Newborn	50	50
4 months	40	60
Young Adult	25	75
Old Age	15	85

Older adults may see their REM sleep to drop at paltry 15 percent. Old age shows an overall reduction in total sleep time with a decrease in both REM and the deeper NREM (slow wave sleep), with an increase in lighter NREM sleep. That is why older adults often complain of tiredness and not getting enough sleep even if they spend enough time in bed.

The cause of sleep architecture and its age-related changes remains a scientific mystery. But there are ways to counter some the age-related sleep difficulties. Chief among them is exercise will increase the percentage of deep restorative sleep. We will learn more about them in the section on Sleep Strategies.

Chapter 3

HOW MUCH SLEEP DO WE NEED?

We spend about a third of our lives in sleep. Sleep along with nutrition and exercise is necessary for healthy living. As a culture, we value hard work, productivity, and efficiency. Americans work long hours, take less vacation, and sleep fewer hours compared to people in many developed nations. Surveys have shown that around one-third of the US population may be suffering from one or more sleep problems such as difficulty initiating or maintaining sleep, waking up too early, and non-restorative or poor quality of sleep. A recent study found that US workers lose 11.3 days of work due to sleep problems. That averages out to 2280 dollars lost per person per year. In total, untreated sleep problems may cost the US economy 63 billion dollars annually.

Sleep is the time when the body does repair work and maintenance. Lack of sleep produces stress in the body. Glucocorticoid is a stress hormone which is secreted by the adrenal glands when we experience stress. This same hormone is also elevated after a single night of disturbed sleep. When we are under pressure, we find it hard to sleep. Thus, a single night of poor sleep can create a vicious cycle of recurring stressors and further sleep deprivation. Lack of sleep impairs with our learning ability and judgment. This further limit our ability to solve problems. Unresolved life problems become a source of stressors and create new sleep issues.

How much sleep does one need?

Our sleep needs change as we grow old. Newborns and children require the most sleep, teenagers also require more sleep than adults, and as we reach adulthood, our sleep needs stabilize. The National Sleep Foundation has the following recommendations:

Life Stage	Age	Sleep-Needs
Newborns	0-3 months	14 to 17 hours
Infants	4 to 11 months	12 to 15 hours
Toddlers	1 to 2 years	11 to 14 hours
Preschoolers	3 to 5 years	10 to 13 hours
School Children	6 to 13 years	9 to 11 hours
Teenagers	14 to 17 years	8 to 10 hours
Young Adults	18 to 25 years	7 to 9 hours
Adults	26 to 64 years	7 to 9 hours
Older adults	65 years and over	7 to 8 hours

These are the guidelines for healthy individuals. A variation from these hours may be unhealthy and suggest a sleep-disorder or a medical illness. Sleep-hours are different from bed-hours because we do not fall asleep as soon as we lie down. There is a time lag between the time we lie down and fall asleep. This time lag is known as sleep latency, and it varies from person to person. Also, we do not get out of bed as soon as wake up. We often spend a few moments in bed before getting up. For many the time in bed before and after sleep is time for contemplation, creativity, and introspection. Many people come up with brilliant ideas while in bed. Also, the time in bed is for relaxing activity like massage, making love. Thus, one should add an extra one to two hours of bed-time depending on one's routine.

Poor sleep quality or quantity can lead to acute and chronic health problems, afflicting the mind and the body. When we get good sleep, our mind performs at its best. We can make the best decisions using the available information. The brain becomes adept at dealing with daily stressors and setbacks.

Mental problems with Sleep Deprivation:

The brain uses neurotransmitters to think, remember, analyze and experience emotions. Neurotransmitters are depleted as the day goes on and are regenerated during sleep. People with chronic sleep deprivation may have depleted neurotransmitters which may trigger psychiatric symptoms. A person that does not sleep for days may experience a psychotic or a manic episode. Also, poor sleep is associated with depression, anxiety, and ADHD symptoms. It may diminish cognition, memory, alertness, creativity and problem-solving abilities.

Many are familiar with the feelings of irritability, distractibility, fatigue, forgetfulness, and inattention following a night-shift. Sleep loss endangers not only the individual but also the community. Someone who has not slept for 24 hours is as impaired as someone who is drunk with high blood alcohol level above 0.08% (more than the legal limit in the USA). It can lead to slower reaction time, reduced vigilance and deficits in information processing which increases the risk for motor vehicle accidents. The National Highway Traffic Safety Administration attributes around 100,000 police reported crashes as the direct result of driver fatigue each year.

Physical problems with sleep deprivation:

Sleep looks quiescent, but it's highly productive for mind and body. Sleep is the time for our body's rest and restoration. Many hormonal changes take place. The pituitary secretes Growth hormone which is essential for growth and development. The Pineal gland secretes Melatonin which is a powerful antioxidant and a scavenger of free radicals.

Melatonin is also anti-inflammatory and plays a crucial role in tissue repair and healing. The stress hormone cortisol drops at bedtime and helps us relax and unwind. The immune system becomes active during sleep, and kills germs, fights tumors, and removes toxins. Sleep also regulates the hormones leptin and ghrelin which controls our hunger and satiety .

Lack of sleep impairs the body's glucose metabolism and increases the craving for high-calorie food. The above physiological findings are supported by clinical research which has linked sleep deprivation to obesity, hypertension, diabetes and heart attack. Poor sleep has been shown to reduce immunity along with an increased incidence of cancer and infections. Even a single night of lost sleep increases one's chance of catching a common cold.

Sleep loss accelerates the aging process, making the body vulnerable to many maladies. Fortunately, simple lifestyle adjustments can help sleep.

Chapter 4

SLEEP REGULATION & INSOMNIA

Sleep and Wake are regulated by the interplay of two opposite processes like the yin and yang. Scientists Borbely and Acherman postulated this two-process model in 1999. The process works separately in the opposite direction. Process C pushes us to stay awake, and process S helps us to fall asleep.

Processes S: Sleep Homeostatic Drive (Sleep drive)
Processes C: Circadian Arousal drove (Wake drive)

For simplicity, I will be referring to these processes as the Sleep Drive and Wake drive.

Sleep drive works as a function of the sleep deprivation. The longer we stay awake, the stronger the urge to fall asleep. Thus, the sleep drive increases in proportion to the time we stay awake. The sleep drive is minimal in the morning after a good night sleep, and maximal in the evening and night after a hard day's labor.

The Wake drive is a function of the Circadian rhythm. Wake drive is high during the daytime and slowly diminishes at night. Light and darkness regulate wake drive.

In perfect harmony, Wake drive keeps us alert and active during the daytime, and slowly diminishes at dusk, and fades away at night like the sunset. Sleep drive remains week at the beginning of the day, and gradually increases and takes over when wake dive fades at night. Many sleep problems ensue when this harmony is lost.

Insomnia is the medical term for severe sleep problems. Sleeplessness or Insomnia is a disease where people have trouble falling asleep, staying asleep, or waking too early, resulting in daytime impairment. It can be temporary for a short period or may linger longer. Based on the problem it is classified as

INSOMNIA SUBTYPES:

Early: Taking too time to get to sleep

Middle: Waking up or interrupted sleep in the middle or throughout the night

Terminal: Early morning awakenings and inability to go to bed after that

Transient: Short-term, often a result of a temporary change in sleep environment, usually resolving within a week

Acute: Insomnia lasting from one week to one month

Chronic: Insomnia lasting for more than one month

Primary: Not due to any medical or psychiatric or environmental cause

Secondary: Due to a medical or psychiatric or environmental causes

Initially, insomnia was thought to be a symptom of an underlying problem or imbalance. The current trend is to regard insomnia as a disease by itself and to get away from the primary and secondary paradigm. The emphasis is to take insomnia seriously as a disease by itself. Because of its potential to cause problems in all domains of health and activity, insomnia is considered a primary disease entity by itself.

The latest Diagnostic and Statistical Manual V (DSM V) of psychiatry has removed primary insomnia (insomnia alone) and secondary insomnia (insomnia due to a medical condition) from the manual. Instead, now Insomnia as a disorder stands alone with its own set of criterions irrespective of the cause.

The DSM-V criteria for Insomnia:

Predominant complaint of dissatisfaction with sleep quantity or quality, associated with one (or more) of the following symptoms:

Difficulty in initiating sleep. (In children, this may manifest as difficulty starting sleep without caregiver intervention.)

Difficulty maintaining sleep, characterized by frequent awakenings or problems returning to sleep after awakenings. (In children, this may manifest as difficulty returning to sleep without caregiver intervention.)

Early-morning awakening with inability to return to sleep.

In addition, the sleep disturbance causes clinically significant distress or impairment in social, occupational, educational, academic, behavioral, or other critical areas of functioning.

The sleep difficulty occurs at least three nights per week. The sleep difficulty is present for at least three months. The sleep difficulty occurs despite adequate opportunity for sleep.

Chapter 5

PHASES OF SLEEP

We think of regular sleep as a continuous, uninterrupted stretch of 7 to 8 hours at night. Sleeping as a single phase of time is a recent phenomenon. Historically, people have got their sleep in two phases or sometimes in three phases depending on the weather and their schedule.

Life has changed with industrialization. The three cardinal aspects of health: food, activity, and sleep have been altered. In the pre-industrialized society and even today in places without access to electric light, human sleep pattern is different. We are all used to the idea of having a sound sleep in one single block lasing eight hours or so. Any deviation to this is considered an anomaly and lumped as a sleep problem or insomnia. However unbelievable it may sound; these eight hours of concentrated monophasic sleep has not been the historical norm.

If we look back, even a hundred years ago, we find that electric light was unavailable in most parts of the world, and even when it was available, it was expensive, and out of reach for the majority. People were exposed to long dark periods at night especially during winter in temperate regions. They went to bed early as the artificial light was a rare and precious commodity. Historian Roger Ekirch has collected historical data from many centuries which shows that sleep at night primarily consisted of two parts. The first part started a few hours after sunset around 8 P.M. and lasted for around four hours. The first sleep was followed by a second sleep starting from 2 A.M. till the sunrise. The period between two sleeps consisted of one to two hours.

People were awake at this time in a very relaxed state. This wake time was considered important, and people used in various ways. Some prayed, some thought about their dreams, some talked, poets composed poems, some visited their neighbors, some had sex and some committed crimes. The sleep intermission time was a common occurrence during winter in the temperate regions where there is a period of 14-hours of darkness. Roger Ekirch found the reference of this biphasic sleep in various languages like French, English, Italian, English, Greek (Homeric Epic) and even among Tiv group of Central Nigeria.

We know that human physiology has remained the same since the last 40,000 years from the time the first Cro-Magnon people made the cave paintings. Does it also pertain to our sleep pattern and if yes, in what ways? To answer this, Thomas Wehr conducted a landmark experiment in which he mimicked the conditions of a temperate winter of the past. He invited a group of volunteers to sleep at night. Seven volunteers were exposed to 14 hours of darkness and ten hours of light as would be expected in the cold temperate winters. No electric light nor any music or TV was allowed. Initially, they all slept for 11 hours every night, probably catching up on their lost sleep.

After some time, something exciting began to happen. Volunteers started to get up in the middle of the night for a few hours, they thought about their dreams and lives, chatted and talked with others, and then went back to sleep. Their sleep was divided into two distinct phases at night with a 1 to

3 hour of wakefulness in between, instead of a single big chunk that we generally associate with good night sleep. Thus, their sleep converted to the pre-industrialized pattern of sleep with two 4 hours blocks interspersed with 1-2 hours of awakening.

Thus, it seems that if given a chance our body will split the sleep into roughly two equal parts at night leading to a biphasic sleep and sometimes a small nap at daytime leading to a triphasic pattern of sleep. This sleep partitions may sound radical, but this is natural sleep phenomenon. Doctors should keep these different sleep patterns into consideration during all assessment and treatment of insomnia.

Many people who get up in the middle of the night worrying that something might be wrong. In some cases, getting up in the middle of the night is normal. They might just be responding to the body's natural sleep rhythm. The problem happens only when they cannot go back to sleep. Failure to fall back to sleep may indicate insomnia.

Many patients when they cannot sleep through the night, will get up, watch some TV, or read. The light exposure will disrupt the natural sleep rhythm. As we know bright light primarily in the blue spectrum inhibits the melatonin. The body will mistake the bright light at night with the sunlight of the daytime. The bright light will activate the wake drive process making it difficult to go back to sleep. In the pre-industrialized societies, people were not exposed to bright artificial light in the middle of the night. Their eyes and bodies still bathed in the darkness of night as they chatted, contemplated about their dreams, had sex, and did other activities generally permitted at dark. Thus, their body was able to remain in sync with the Circadian clock, and as a result, they were able to go back to sleep again and complete the second block of sleep.

The understanding of a biphasic sleep pattern is essential both for the clinicians and their clients. Biphasic sleep may be misdiagnosed as middle insomnia. Middle insomnia is the difficulty of returning to sleep after waking up during the night or very early in the morning. It is also called nocturnal awakenings, middle of the night awakenings, sleep maintenance insomnia. This kind of insomnia is different from initial or sleep-onset insomnia, which consists of having difficulty falling asleep at the beginning of sleep. One must be careful to distinguish the two as biphasic sleep is a normal physiological sleep pattern, whereas insomnia is pathological and may be a symptom of a serious illness. Let us analyze the case of Brian who came to with sleep problems in the middle of the night?

Brian is a divorced middle-aged man who works a regular 9 to 5 job. He lives alone with his dog. He goes to bed early at 8 pm as a part of his lifelong habit instilled in childhood by his dad. He used to do fine but for the past few years – he is waking up in the middle of the night. He was able to go back to sleep sometimes but recently cannot seem to do so. He has read on the internet that the bed should only be used for sleep and if you cannot sleep – you should get up, move around, may read or watch TV and stay out of bed till you fall asleep again. He had followed that advice but cannot go back to sleep. He lays awake from the middle of the night till the morning. He feels tired and miserable, and his work is suffering. What can be done to help Brian?

Advice for Brian:

Many people like Brian may be merely exhibiting the natural biphasic sleep pattern and may not have insomnia. As a conservative first line of treatment, the first step may be re-assurance and sleep-coaching. Sometimes the worry of having an abnormal sleep, and the fear of not able to go back to sleep becomes a self-fulfilling prophecy. I educated Brian about the biphasic sleep and the importance of sleep hygiene. Brian was encouraged to stay in his bed for a while after he wakes up and thinks about his dreams or other thoughts that come to his mind.

Brian can get up and read something or write something using a dim non-blue light lamb. Since most CFL bulbs are high in white and blue light, they disrupt the sleep the most. I advised Brian to get a low power incandescent light for his lamp or wrap his lamp with a red cloth, which will shift the spectrum more towards a red light. And to avoid all other types of lights. He should again go to bed and attempt to sleep within an hour.

He came to see me after a month. He looked happy and well rested. He said that he was sleeping well. He felt less anxious about falling back to sleep after my sleep-coaching and reassurances. He sometimes struggles to go back to sleep on a few nights, but for the majority, he is either sleeping through the night or able to go back to sleep after an hour of quiet awakening.

If Bran had continued to fail to fall asleep in the second half, despite all the cognitive, behavioral and environmental modifications, then he probably had a more serious condition. It will be more likely a case of abnormal middle insomnia than normal biphasic sleep and warrants a medical workup. In conclusion, both patients and physicians need to be aware of the natural biphasic sleep pattern which is distinct from middle insomnia and should be treated accordingly. Any case of middle-insomnia should be analyzed in detail to rule out the possibility of a biphasic sleep pattern which is normal. Sleep medications should always be the last resort after all conservative measures have failed.

PART II
IMPORTANCE OF SLEEP

Chapter 6

SLEEP HEALING IN ANCIENT TIMES

Sleep has many health benefits. Every organ system benefits from sleep. All bodily functions do better with sleep. No matter what the disease is, sleep always helps in the healing. Once the disease process sets in, sleep may not cure it, but lack of sleep will invariably worsen the disease. Sleep boosts immunity and helps in the fight against, bacteria, virus, and carcinogens. Modern science has just begun to unravel the myriad benefits of sleep.

The health benefits of sleep were also realized in the ancient times. The use of sleep as healing is as old as healing itself. The first hospitals in the world were Sleep hospitals. If we define 'hospital' as a place devoted to healing and curing ailments, then the distinction of the first hospital will go to Egyptian healing (sleeping) temples built by Imhotep.

Imhotep who lived around 2600 BC was the physician, chief minister, and priest to the Pharaoh Djoser. He was glamorized in the movie The Mummy. He was a great architect and credited with building the first pyramid. People from all over the Nile came to these temples for healing. Patients went through ritual ablutions and were put to sleep through hypnotic suggestions by the priests.

The idea was that, while people are sleeping, the gods will give the answer to the ills and speak through the dreams. Hence, great emphasis was placed on the content of the dreams as they were thought to contain the means of cure and healing. Priest and priestess would interpret, analyze the dreams and give people answers.

The Egyptians influenced the ancient Greek culture. With time, the practice of sleep-healing-temples became popular in Greece. Healing temples were built in honor of Asclepius, the Greek god of healing and medicinal arts. The temples were known as Asklepian and became popular places of healing. People from far flocked to seek a remedy for their illness. Like the Egyptian temples, all healing was believed to take place while the person was sleeping.

The deep sleep was induced through a trance by the chanting and suggestion of the priests. The person will lay there in sleep or trance for around three days called the incubation period. Many times, non-venomous snakes, considered sacred, will crawl on the floor of the temple where the sick slept. The use of snake was deemed to be necessary for healing. This role of the snake was depicted by the attributes of God Asclepius who had the snake and the staff- also called the Rod of Asclepius.

The sleep temples did not distinguish between mental, physical and the spiritual. People from all walks came with all kinds of illness- some seeking a cure for their illness, some seeking answers, and some with psychological conflicts. Many patients got well, and the word spread. People kept on coming back, and the temples became very popular, and they were built in other parts of Greece.

The most famous sleep temple was at Epidaurus built around 420 BC. Another renowned temple was located on the island of Kos, where Hippocrates, the father of medicine began his career around 400 BC. The basic premise remained the same: the seeker will come, perform the rituals and sacrifices, get a suggestion and go into a trance like sleep. They will wake up after many hours or days, tell their dreams. There was a belief that God will be healing and answering in dreams which will be interpreted by the priests.

The Romans, who succeeded the Greeks, adopted the sleep temples and dedicated them to God Apollo. Similar practices also used by the Hebrews and other cultures. In India, there were practices somewhat similar in concept but different in practice like the Yoga-Nidra which was believed to have healing powers.

When we examine these ancient practices, it will be naïve to dismiss all that was done as superstition. Any custom that lasted for over a thousand years must serve some purpose. All the evidence we have of the time and practice are from the archeology and ancient texts. We can never ascertain how much of actual healing took place.

I believe the healing mainly took place during the period of rest, sleep, relaxation. The sick was free from any work or family obligations. The sick was allowed to be sick without stigma. The body has rejuvenating powers. Enough rest, nutrition and a therapeutic milieu can rejuvenate the body. But, we can be confident that all illness was not cured then, as is now.

The chanting and hypnotic suggestions of the priests and the sacred atmosphere of the temple, with all the prayers, must have played a robust therapeutic placebo effect, harnessing all of the body's power to heal itself. I suspect that the strong faith in the healers and healing worked in combination with the rest and relaxation restored the body to an earlier healthier state.

In summary, sleep is vital for life and longevity. Ancient healing traditions regularly harnessed the healing powers of sleep. In the industrial age, when productivity and industry were valued above all, sleep became associated with sloth. This unfortunate connotation misguided many people including both the physicians and patients leading to a modern society where people are sleep deprived, fatigued and overworked.

Fortunately, albeit late, modern medicine has begun to catch up with the life-giving powers of sleep. Sleep has now been restored to one of the three pillars of health along with nutrition and exercise.

And, regarding ancient sleep-temples, we still carry its legacy in modern medical practices. Physicians upon completion of their medical training across the world swear their Hippocratic Oath on the name of gods Apollo and Asclepius. The Hippocratic oath begins with: "I swear by Apollo, the Physician and by Asclepius and by Hygieia and Panacea and by all the gods ..." Additionally, the rod of Asclepius" is used by many medical associations across the world as a symbol for medicine. If you have ever wondered, why there is a picture of a snake and stick sitting in your doctor's office or on the hospital-wall, you now have the answer.

Chapter 7

UNDERSTANDING DREAMS

People have been fascinated with dreams since the dawn of civilization. Dreams formed an important part in pre-agricultural and pre-industrial societies. There have been reports of native Indian tribes using their dreams to guide them in choosing leaders. The Egyptians who built the first hospitals used dreams for treatments. People who were suffering from mental and physical ailments used to go to the temples where they would get suggestions (hypnotic) and sleep. They would get up from their sleep and share their dreams with the priests and priestess who were the official dream interpreters. The idea was to let God speak through the dreams and tell the solution to the person's ailment. Soon sleep temples aka dream temples aka healing temples aka hospitals spread over Greece, Rome and other parts of the world. By the success and longevity of the practice, it seems the process helped some if not all.

The first serious study of a dream in modern times was conducted by Sigmund Freud (1856-1939). He is considered the father of dream research and psychoanalysis. He used hypnosis to unravel the hidden thoughts of the mind and treat patients suffering from various ailments. Freud asserted that our unconscious also influences our thoughts and actions. Freud was influenced by Darwin. He believed that the urges of sex and aggression are part of the being but are repressed in the modern society and stored in the unconscious. This repression is the root cause of many mental and physical ailments.

Freud believed that understanding the unconscious will give the key to understand the hidden, repressed urges, and their healthy release will lead to recovery. For some time, he dabbled with hypnosis using a drug called amyl nitrate, but later on, give up on that. He discovered something called the free association where a patient will sleep on a couch, relax, close their eyes and speak whatever first comes to their mind. The doctor will say a word and patient will say the first thing that comes to their mind- thus the term free-association.

Freud believed that dreams held the keys to understanding the unconscious. Dream analysis and their interpretation became a fundamental part of the psychoanalytic therapy. Freud believed that the contents of the dream are symbolic of some higher truth about the person. The unconscious is communicating through symbols and metaphors, and many innocuous themes may have sinister meanings. Like a cigar in a dream can be a symbol of the penis and the urge to smoke can be seen as a means to accomplish unfulfilled orality. For many years, Freudian thought dominated the modern understanding of dreams and psychiatric thinking.

However, a big fallacy of the Freudian method was that it was unverifiable. Many of his theories are impossible to prove or disprove. The latter part of the twentieth century saw many inventions which gave us a direct picture of the mind in action. There was no longer a need to rely on speculations about symbols and dream metaphors. Inventions like EEG, PET scan, and MRI, revolutionized our understanding of the brain function and its processes.

The question, however, why we dream, and its purpose has continued to baffle scientists. As for its meanings, many researchers have studied thousands of dreams. Modern dream theory as propagated by scientists Hobson & McCarley, Fiss and others, demystifies the process of dreams and rejects the notion of any higher power or higher meaning. It seems that dreams are not that mystical at all. Dreams are not messages from the past nor a prediction of future. There may be some dreams with greater meaning than what meets the eye, but most dreams are ordinary and "what you see, that you get to type."

You dream whatever is occupying your mind at that time. For example, if you are about to start a new job and dream that you are lost in an unknown place and cannot find your way home, the dream is a manifestation about the anxiety you are feeling at being at the new job, new pace, new co-workers and related stress.

Similarly, if you are about to go on a date (more with first) and the previous night you dream that you have spilled coffee on your shirt and ruined your dress, it may just be you are anxious about putting up a good impression. Many times, people fret about higher meaning and a more complicated explanation when the solution is simple and agrees with your current life situation.

The allure and appeal of mystical dreams are fueled by stories and folktales we hear about dreams when growing up. There are legends of queens dreaming strange symbols which were interpreted as an omen of progeny's greatness by their courtiers. On the night of the conception of Buddha, his mother Queen Maya dreamt of a white elephant with six white tusks entered her right side. Courtiers interpreted that Buddha will either be the greatest King or the greatest Seer.

Similarly, historian Plutarch reports that queen Olympias had a bizarre dream on the night before her consummation of marriage with King Philip. She dreamt that "there was a peal of thunder and that a thunderbolt fell upon her womb, and that thereby much fire was kindled, which broke into flames that traveled all about, and then was extinguished." At a later time too after the marriage, Philip dreamed that he was putting a seal upon his wife's womb; and the device of the seal, as he thought, was the figure of a lion. Folklores like this later led to the myth of Alexander being the son of God Zeus.

People may question, well some people got higher messages in their dreamlike Abraham Lincoln who dreamt about his death weeks before his assassination. However, if we carefully study the facts, we will see that there were attacks made or planned on the life of Abraham Lincoln, and at that precarious moment of civil war, it was not that unexpected. Lincoln was worried about the war and dangers to his own life. His unconscious mind was studying the situation in the backdrop and showed him that scenario as a probability in his dreams.

Chapter 8

HEALTH BENEFITS OF DREAM

The answer to why we dream remains a mystery with multiple explanations. Dreams may help us in various mental processes and functions. But dreams can harm too. Here are three ways dream enhance our brain function-

Dreams help with learning and memory.

Sleep plays a vital role in memory and learning. As we discussed before, sleep can be of two types. Slow wave sleep (NREM) and dream sleep (REM). Sleep, especially the dream sleep helps in memory and learning. All the information we get during the day is organized and filed during our dreams. Unnecessary information is discarded, and associations are made. One of the common side effects of alcohol and benzodiazepine class of drugs is the loss of dream (REM) sleep. One significant side effect of these drugs is a loss of memory and impairment of new learning.

Dream help in problem-solving.

Have you noticed that before making important decisions, many people prefer to take time and sleep on it? This delay seems to help the decision-making process as you let your unconscious mind work on the problem overnight. Many times, when you get up in the morning, you get an insight which was missed before. It has led to the idea that dreams play a key role in problem-solving. Many times, during the day, we get distracted by multiple stimuli and information overload. During sleep, we can synthesize this information and make sense of them.

Dreams alert us about trauma.

Sometimes we get premonitions about some incoming dangers or events in our dreams. The unconscious brain many times can connect the dots before our conscious mind realizes it. This power of the unconscious is the basis of dream analysis as practiced since ancient times. However true premonitions are very rare. , Most of our dreams are about the trauma which has already happened to us. Nightmares about trauma and adverse events remind and alert us about those dangers. It may be a way to coax us to take the required remedial steps. For example, if a dog once bites you, you may dream of a dog chasing you.

When are dreams harmful?

Although dreams about trauma serve a biological function, they are not always desirable. In my practice, I see people suffering from post-traumatic stress disorder often replay their trauma in their dreams. Many soldiers coming back from Iraq and Afghanistan have reported to me their traumatic experiences which they relive in their dreams. Same also happens with accident and rape victims. Dreams may become be a way for the body to cope with the trauma and alerting the body about the dangers of injury. But these dreams disrupt the sleep and increases the sufferings of the patients. I use medications like Prazosin which dampen the fight or flight response and reduce the intensity and frequency of these dreams.

How to harness the power of dreams?

Dreams occur when we are in the REM stage of sleep. In dreams, we are experiencing the things happening to us. Out logical brain is put under suspension, but our unconscious mind is working hard to connect the dots. Thus, dreams can be a tool for higher creativity. Many great people have attributed their discoveries to their dreams. For example, the Indian mathematical genius Srinivasa Ramanujan without receiving any formal training solved over 3000 equations during his short life of 39 years. He would say that a Goddess named Namakkal would appear in his dreams and showed him the solutions.

Many modern authors have attributed their story idea and plots to their dreams. Notable among them are Stephen King for his books; and Stephen Myer for her Twilight series.

During writing this book, I got many ideas and insights in my dreams. But it was a deliberate effort. The whole day, I have been thinking about some point I want to mention in the book, and the best way to shape the argument. I was thinking about this before I went to bed. In the morning, I would be surprised with new answers. Many dots which my conscious mind could not solve, were connected in my sleep by my unconscious.

Before you go to sleep every night, try to think about any question or problem you are seeking answers. Or just anything that you want to accomplish soon. Now as you roll into sleep, your brain will keep working on the problem. In the REM state of sleep, the brain is working hard as if it's awake. The unconscious mind will try to connect the dots and dreams play an active role in this creative process. When you get up in the morning, many times (not always) you will be amazed to find new insights. It is an excellent practice to sleep with paper and pen or tape recorder, as many creative people have realized their best idea; the first thing they get up in the morning.

Below is a list of some of the great ideas inspired by dreams:

Dream Discoveries

Dreamer	Dreams
Mary Shelley	Frankenstein's Monster
Dmitri Mendeleev	The arrangement of elements in the Periodic table
Stephenie Meyer	Girl in love with a vampire: Subject of twilight saga
Jack Nicklaus	Correct grip for his golf swing
Paul McCartney	Song: "yesterday."
Elias Howe	Eye of the needle in the sewing machine
Friedrich August Kekulé	Structure of Benzene Ring
Srinivasa Ramanujan	Mathematical Theorems
Stephen King	The idea of novel Misery, Dream Catcher
Niels Bohr	Structure of Atom
Otto Loewi	Nerve Impulse Breakthrough
Rene Descartes	Four rules of skepticism as a scientific method

Christopher Nolan	The idea for the movie Inception
John Lennon	Song: #9 Dream
James Cameron	Ideas for Terminator and Avatar
Salvador Deli	Painting "Persistence of Memory"
Louis Agassiz	Structure of Fossil Fish
H. P. Lovecraft	The book: Necronomicon

Chapter 9

BENEFITS OF NAP

A nap is a planned short sleep taken during the daytime in addition to the regular night sleep. Napping has a bad reputation and stigma attached to it. Many feel that any adult napping in the daytime is a sign of laziness, lack of ambition and low standards. Some believe that naps will lead to weight gain and obesity. Napping is thought to be right only for the children, the elderly and the sick.

In the scorching heat of summer, outdoor temperatures in many parts can go near 100 degrees Fahrenheit. Working outdoors stretches the limit of human capacity. People in the tropics traditionally have taken naps during this period and resumed work again when the temperature is more forgiving. Now we mostly work indoors, with indoor air conditioning. There are many myths and confusion surrounding naps. Does nap have any role in our modern society? Let us find out.

As a society, we value efficiency and productivity above all. We are all impressed by the workhorses who manage to pull off night-long-work effortlessly to finish class assignments or complete work projects. When employers say, they want flexible and open-minded hard workers, what they want is employees who can burn the candle both ends to get the work done and yet keep a smile. When people are trying to minimize night-time sleep to have more action and fun, the talk about an afternoon nap will raise eyebrows.

Culturally napping is more prevalent among people in tropical and Mediterranean climate. Siesta or the post-lunch-nap is a common practice to escape the hot afternoons and work more in the cooler evenings. When I was growing up in Kolkata, India, it was usual to see manual laborers, shop-keepers, pedestrians napping under big trees' shades in the noon. However, I see it less and less when I visit India now. I guess it's a part of the broader global trend as more the economy is modernized, the lesser the people have time for naps.

The industrial revolution began in Western Europe. The colonial powers dominated the world with their advanced technology, increased productivity and the modern economy. The industrial powerhouse of western Europe namely, Britain and Germany have long cold winters. In these cold, dreary winters, napping in the daytime is a waste of the precious light and heat freely supplied by the sun for a few hours. The traditional 9 to 5 pm work schedule suits best in that climate.

Other cultures with hot weather traditionally had a big afternoon meal followed by a long nap or siesta and then return to work afterward. In the absence of air-conditioning, a nap is still the best way to beat the heat. However, within the modern global economy, most cultures irrespective of weather are switching to a 9 to 5 work routine with hopes of higher growth and productivity.

History, however, is replete with many successful people who harnessed the power of naps to boost their productivity. Many American Presidents like Ronald Reagan, Bill Clinton, John F Kennedy, Lyndon Johnson, George W Bush all took naps. John F Kennedy famously ate his lunch in bed and took one to two hours of a nap every day in a clean dark room.

Some other historical figures like Winston Churchill, Margaret Thatcher, Napoleon Bonaparte, Thomas Edison, Leonardo Da Vinci, Albert Einstein and John D Rockefeller were also known to take planned naps. Most of these people were highly productive and were known to work long hours extending to late nights.

During World War II, Winston Churchill would nap religiously for at least an hour every afternoon. He would wake up refreshed and be able to work long nights and ultimately lead the allied powers to victory. He famously said "Nature had not intended mankind to work from eight in the morning until midnight without the refreshment of blessed oblivion which, even if it only lasts 20 minutes, is sufficient to renew all the vital forces".

Let us now keep the culture and history aside and look at what science says about napping. Our sleep and wake are regulated by the body's internal biological rhythm also known as the Circadian rhythm. The Circadian clock helps us stay awake. However, the wake drive varies throughout the day. The circadian clock rises and dips at a different rate during the day. That is why most people experience a different level of alertness throughout the day.

We feel the strongest urge to sleep between 2:00-4:00 am at night. Surprisingly, the second strongest call for sleep is about 12 hours later in the afternoon around 2 to 4 pm commonly knows a "post-lunch-dip." That means we are biologically wired to crave for the afternoon nap. Another thing to note is even with a full night of rest; people will feel more alert at 6 pm than at 3 pm. This mid-afternoon slump is independent of the time and the amount of food intake. These Circadian dips of intense sleepiness will be even more if we are sleep deprived. Moreover, the timing of the afternoon dip (2 to 4 pm) can be earlier for morning person and later for evening persons.

Thus, we can see that there is a natural drive towards afternoon nap in most of us. Many of us avert this by drinking coffee, energy drinks or soda. Some of us move around, chat, watch or read something interesting on screen or paper; we do anything to keep those sleep demons away. Then in a matter of few hours irrespective of what we have done during those 2 to 4 pm hours, our Circadian clock makes us alert again.

Research has shown that taking a nap during the post-lunch-dip is good for us. Nap is the best thing to do for health and productivity. Afternoon nap (siesta) is associated with a 37 percent reduction in coronary mortality. This means that regular nappers have a decreased chance of getting a heart attack. It may be due to a decrease in stress levels, along with a reduction in blood pressure and heart rate during naps.

Many people have experienced more tiredness and sleepiness following a nap. People have complained of feeling sleepier after the nap. Some have felt cognitive dullness and disorientation. On the other hand, regular die-hard nappers will swear for nap's effectiveness and how refreshed, revitalized and happy it makes them feel. Why is this difference in experience? To understand this, we need a closer look at the sleep cycle. Not all naps are created equal.

During sleep, we switch between NREM and REM states in cycles lasting approximately 90 minutes each. Each night we experience between 4 to 6 sleep cycles on average. Each sleep cycle proceeds in predictable order from light sleep->deep sleep->Dream sleep. Every time we attempt to sleep-whether it's for a daytime nap or nighttime sleep, the body goes through the same sequence of stages. It takes approximately 90 minutes to complete one cycle.

Each stage has its benefits. Maximum refreshing occurs when the body can complete one full cycle comprising all the three stages. Below is an approximate timeline of the first sleep cycle showing the total time spent in each stage.

NREM: Light Sleep	25 – 35 minutes
NREM: Deep Sleep	20- 40 minutes
REM: Dream Sleep	10-15 minutes

A nap can be of two types depending on duration: a short nap and a long nap. The short nap is also known as a power nap or cat-nap. It generally lasts around 20-30 minutes. The short nap only covers the light stage of NREM sleep and ends before the deep stage. Many people prefer a short nap in the middle of a busy day as there is no associated grogginess after waking up. A power nap can make people feel more alert, revitalized with improved mental and motor performance. The other good thing about power nap is that it does not interfere with night's sleep. Power naps are ideal when you have regular workday with limited time and need peak performance immediately after waking up.

he long naps usually last anywhere from more than 30

minutes to a few hours. A long nap will invariably extend to the deepest stage of NREM when the brain has slow waves. In the stage, all the blood is drained out of the brain to the muscles. Maximum muscle recovery happens in this stage. However, if someone is wakened up in the deep stage they will feel considerable sleep inertia. Sleep inertia is a physiological state when the body is transitioning from sleep to wakefulness. It happens immediately after waking and the individual experiences drowsiness, disorientation and a decline in motor function.

Sleep inertia is more pronounced when you are woken by someone or the alarm clock before the ninety-minute cycle. Sometimes you will wake up in the middle of a vivid dream while you are REM sleep, or muscle paralysis if in slow wave sleep. For next 5 to 30 minutes (individually variable), you may feel little groggy, disoriented and will want to go back to sleep again as your body is adjusting to the waking state from the sleep state. Do not worry as this is temporary.

Once we overcome the sleep inertia, long naps are more beneficial than short naps. The body will soon be awake with renewed vigor and energy. However, sleep inertia makes the longer naps less suitable for those who need to have peak performance immediately after waking up. Longer naps have many advantages. If you are on to shift work or plan to pull an all-nighter for the exam, or recovering from a jet-lag, or recapitulating from sleep deprivation, the long naps can be beneficial.

As a doctor, I have to take care of patients at night. During those night works, I always try to get a nap before. When given a chance, I would come back home little early and try to get a good long nap before the night was about to start. The days, I could get my nap, the nights seemed much easier and I felt less tired and groggy. Research has validated the finding and shown that people working all night are more active and make fewer errors if allowed a nap before.

Many studies have looked into the effects of nap duration and its impact. Chief among them are funded by the National Aeronautics and Space Administration (NASA) and National Institute of Mental Health (NIMH). NASA regularly sends astronauts for space travel.

The Astronauts traveling in space struggle with sleep due to irregular light and dark exposure. They on average get two hours of less sleep in Space compared to Earth. This has prompted NASA to conduct multiple research on sleep and napping. The NASA study led by David F. Dinges looked at 91 volunteers who spent 10 days living on one of 18 different sleep schedules. The sleep schedules examined daily naps ranging from 0 to 2.5 hours.

They found that naps improved working memory crucial for pilots running spaceship. The other important finding was that long naps were more effective than short ones. Another NASA study led by Mark Rosekind found that 40-minute rest period provided to pilots improved their performance by 34% and alertness 100%.

The pilots took on average 5-6 minutes to fall asleep and slept for 25.8 minutes. The study is often misquoted in media as 26-minute power nap taken by pilots improved performance. It has to be noted that 26 minutes of sleep came from 40 minutes of the rest period.

Other researchers also found that 45 minutes of nap improved alertness for 6 hours after the nap. Another study found that 1-hour nap sustained alertness for 10 hours. Thus, it seems that the benefits of long naps last longer. Longer naps are thus ideal if one needs to maintain alertness and performance late through the night. Shift workers including doctors are encouraged to take prophylactic long naps before all-night shifts.

The other study funded by NIMH found that midday nap reverses information overload. The amount of information an average worker has to deal on a daily basis has skyrocketed. In this information age, our work demands to analyze and to manipulate big chunks of data. Strenuous mental work exhausts the brain neurotransmitters which are chemicals by which brain cells communicate with each other. Sleep (nap) allows the brain to rest and re-synthesize the neurotransmitters. It means the brain is re-charging its battery during the nap.

In an NIMH study, people were given a visual task on the computer screen. With time, performances dropped, and participants felt burn-out towards the last sessions. However, when they took a 30-minute nap, they could sustain their performance without further deterioration. When allowed a 1-hour to nap their performance improved and their last session was as good as the first (morning) session.

Another NIMH study compared the effects of coffee with a 60-90-minute nap. The nappers outperformed the coffee drinkers in motor skills, perceptual learning, and word recall. Thus, given a choice, a nap will improve performance better than coffee. Another study showed that 60-90 minutes' nap containing both deep slow wave sleep and REM sleep may be as good as an 8-hour sleep for learning complicated tasks.

A nap can also protect lives by lowering your risks of heart attacks. The siesta habit was found to be associated with a 37 percent reduction in coronary mortality. The study done on Greek people found that those who napped occasionally has a 12 percent reduction in coronary mortality, and those napping regularly had a 37 percent reduction in coronary mortality. It is possibly due to reduced stress and from the decrease in blood pressure and heart rate associated with sleep.

Many successful organizations have woken up to the prospect of napping to boost productivity. Government workers in Seoul, South Korea, are allowed to take afternoon naps for about an hour. Many Japanese firms allow their workers to take a nap. It's a part of the Japanese culture, and they have a term for that called Inemuri. It is the Japanese practice of sleeping on the job. Inemuri literally means, " sleeping while present," and can be a way for an employee to show how hard they are working.

There are nap-saloons for men and women in Japan where you can pay money and rent a cozy cabin for a nap. The nap culture is becoming global. In the New-York city, there is a nap salon where you can literally buy sleep along with reflexology treatment. Napping may be the ultimate solution for the sleep-deprived modern 24x7 culture. Companies like Apple, Facebook, Nike, BASF, Opel, Google, the Huffington Post and Procter & Gamble are providing employees with designated nap facilities.

As the world is slowly waking up to the potential of naps, there are some caveats. Napping although good for almost everything may make depression and insomnia worse. People suffering from clinical depression may feel low after getting up from a nap. Depressed people suffer from sleep disturbance which requires professional help. And, those with insomnia may find it even harder to get sleep at night after an afternoon nap.

Another critical downside for longer naps may be interference with night sleep. As mentioned before, the homeostatic sleep drive is depended on your sleep debt, and thus if you have too much sleep credit, you may not fall asleep at night. However, if you are napping to combat the sleep deprivation, go ahead. Don't worry about long or short, go ahead and give your body as much sleep it seeks. Any sleep is better than no-sleep or reduced sleep.

The biggest problem which deters most people away from naps is the fear of sleep problems at night. Naps can impair nighttime sleep. Children and young people are usually more physically active throughout the day compared to older adults. Even if they nap, their body becomes tired, and they can sleep without difficulty. However, as we grow old, we do less physical work. If you have trouble sleeping at night after naps- there are two solutions.

First, keep your nap very short, no more than 20 minutes. The short naps will not interfere with night sleep. Secondly, if you have more time and decide to take a long nap, go ahead. But then when you wake up, you have to leave the house. Spend time outdoors and go for a walk. Do physical exercise.

Excess energy generated by nap needs to be harnessed for physical work and activity. Mental work and exhaustion will not cut the deal. In the big cities in India, a lot of poor immigrants come from work from nearby countryside. They do hard manual labor through the day. During noon, when it becomes unbearably hot, they rest for an hour or so. They will sleep on the streets, or near a tree shade. Then they wake up and go back to the labor again. So vigorous is their physical work, they face no problem with sleep neither at day nor at night.

Lastly, as I mentioned earlier-the body craves nap at a particular time which may vary from 1 to 3 pm or 2 to 4 pm (or 3 to 5 pm) for different people depending on when you get up in the morning. You can try nap at different times for different duration before finding what works best for you.

Our activity and alertness dips for certain few hours in the mid-day and then again, rises later in the evening. Many people cannot nap before or after a specific time. Some of us have a sweet spot or specific nap-zone. For example, I can only nap between 3 and 4 pm. Beginning nap too late or prolonging it too long may impair sleep at night.

Sleep researcher Dr. Dement advice that staying within our nap zone ensures maximum success for our nap. There are always exceptions. My mother can never sleep during the day, while my father can sleep at any time of the day. I envy those people with the God-gifted ability to nap anywhere for any time without disruption to night's sleep. If you are an effortless napper- power to you. Make full use of your gift. For others, find your nap-zone and sweet nap to all.

Chapter 10

MYTHS ASSOCIATED WITH NAP

Over the last few decades' multiple research has extolled the virtues of sleep and nap. There remain many myths surrounding nap and day time sleep. In the previous chapter, we reviewed the scientific evidence supporting the health benefits of a nap. Here I will discuss the six common myths associated with naps and highlight the truth behind them.

Myth #1: Napping is for babies and the elderly!

Fact: Napping can be beneficial for all especially those engaged in intense mental or physical work. A nap can improve alertness, productivity, and creativity. Naps on weekends can compensate for some of the ill effects of sleep deprivation during the week.

Myth #2: After a nap, I will be sleepier!

Fact: A sleep cycle lasts 90 minutes. If your nap is more than 20 minutes but less than 90 minutes you will feel groggy. This drowsiness after waking up from a short nap is because of the sleep inertia as you are waking up before finishing the sleep cycle. But this is temporary and will go away in 5 to 10 minutes. This break is the best time to have a cup of tea and coffee and get back to activity.

Myth #3: Nap will decrease productivity!

Fact: The benefits of a nap are so powerful that many top

companies like Apple, Amazon, Facebook, and Google are providing nap zones for their workers. A short nap has shown to improve workflow, productivity, and efficiency. Do not check social media or surf net during the break. This will make you more tired. Instead, find a comfortable couch or lay your head down on the desk after lunch for around 20 benefits and reap the benefits. I know one doctor who starts his day at 5 am and sees patients till 5 pm. He has been doing this for the last 30 years. His secret- he naps in his minivan during the break for 30 minutes daily.

Myth #4: Naps cause weight gain!

Fact: Decreased sleep disrupts the hormones regulated with appetite and fat storage. Naps never increase weight. On the contrary, the extra sleep will decrease cravings for high-calorie food and help in weight loss. After a sumptuous lunch, we feel sleepy. This sleepiness is natural as more blood is sent to the abdomen for digestion, and less blood is available for brain work. Nap during that time will facilitate better digestion and absorption of food. Increasing your total sleep is one of the quickest ways to lose weight.

Myth #5: Naps impair night sleep!

Fact: Long naps will delay sleep time at night. This delay is normal, as your body will require less sleep at night if you sleep 1-2 hours during the day. However, many people will find it hard to fall asleep if they nap during the day. If that happens, you need to do physical exercise and spend some time outdoors in the evening. Activity will reset the body and prepare it for sleep again at night.

Myth # 6: Nap will make you lazy!

Fact: Nothing can be further from the truth. A nap will renew your energy and vigor. Many leaders like Churchill, Edison, Napoleon regularly took naps and were the most productive people in history. As we work, we deplete the brain neurotransmitters which was can remake during the sleep. Naps during the day make it possible for you to work long hours without getting tired.

In summary, the health benefits of a nap are well proven. The body has a natural urge to sleep during the mid-day sometime between 1 to 4 pm which may vary. Do not fight this. If your work schedule or workspace allows for nap, take the break. A short nap of 20 minutes may be enough for most. Some may benefit from longer 60 to 90-minute nap. We feel the best when we hit the sweet spot in timing the naps. Either we wake up after 20 minutes and feel powerful with the power nap, or we stay along and complete one entire sleep cycle lasting 90 minutes. If we wake up in between this two-time limit, we risk for waking up in the deepest stage of sleep which invariably results in sleep inertia. Whatever the case, a nap is good for health. It will reduce stress and fatigue. Your mind and body will thank you with improved physical and mental performance.

Chapter 11

SLEEP & LIFESPAN: LESSONS FROM BLUE ZONES

Life and death are an integral part of every existence. There is no guarantee for life, but once born, there is guaranteed death. This has fascinated mankind since time immemorial with questions like Why are we born? Why do we age? And why do we die? Religion, philosophy, spirituality, arts: all fields have explored and sought answers. Science has been trying to answer questions that can be objectively measured like how we age, how to stay healthy, how to avoid diseases and how to live longer.

According to the famous Danish twin studies, our genes determine only 25 percent of how long we live, and the rest 75 percent is determined by our lifestyles. One way to study those lifestyle factors can be to visit places where people are living the longest and healthiest and study their lifestyles. Some researchers have done that, and they have called those regions as Blue Zones. Blue Zones are regions on Earth with the longest life expectancy, disability-free life expectancy or concentration of persons over 100. The concept was first developed by Gianni Pes and Michel Poulain when they studied the cluster of villages with the highest longevity in Sardinia's Nuoro province, Italy in 2004. They drew concentric circles blue circles on the map and began referring to the area inside as Blue Zones.

The work on Blue Zones was extended by Dan Buettner, an American explorer, author, and world-record holder for endurance bicycling. During his bicycling trips, he became interested in demographics and longevity and began his research into " blue zones". Dan Buettner discussed them in his landmark book "The Blue Zones: Lessons for Living Longer from the People Who've Lived the Longest". He identified five Blue Zone spots in:

- Sardinia, Italy (particularly Nuoro province and Ogliastra)
- The Islands of Okinawa, Japan
- Loma Linda, California: among Seventh-day Adventists
- Nicoya Peninsula, Costa Rica
- Ikaria, Greece:

Some of the common elements of longevity identified in the Blue Zones were community and family support, social involvement, regular physical activity, stress-free living, positive outlook, and healthy eating. In addition, one key finding was sleep, the topic of this article. Most centenarians go to bed shortly after sunset and wake with daybreak. They rise with the sun and sleep close to sunset. They spend a lot of time outdoors. They sleep on average 8-10 hours per day. In some places, they take an afternoon nap which imparts additional health benefits.

PART III
CIRCADIAN CLOCK

Chapter 12

WHAT IS CIRCADIAN RHYTHM ?

Each living being has a clock inside which tells us the right time to do certain things to promote survival and reproduction. In the following chapters, we will learn about the internal human clock and how it influences our sleep needs and pattern. The internal clock regulating sleep and wake in human is known as Circadian clock or Circadian rhythm.

Circadian rhythm refers to biological processes that follow a periodicity of about 24 hours. The circadian rhythm is an internal clock that is present inside all living forms. The term circadian comes from the Latin "circa" meaning around, and "dies," meaning day. Earth rotates on its axis every 24 hours which also marks the time for day and night. Life evolved on Earth with this periodicity, and all organism has an internal biological clock which is always running in the background.

The circadian rhythm allows the body to make sense of the changing seasons. It makes the plant flower at specific times. It regulates the sleeping, mating and feeding pattern of animals. The circadian rhythm or the internal clock is always taking feedback from the environment and adjusting itself. Each organ in the human body has their own clock, all of which are also regulated by a master clock. In human, this master clock is located in the brain in a region called the hypothalamus as a distinct group of nerve cells called the suprachiasmatic nucleus (SCN).

The SCN receives the information through the eyes. When light enters the retina, it reacts with a pigment called melanopsin, which then sends the information on day and night to the SCN in the hypothalamus. From there, it passes it to the pineal gland located at the center of the brain. The pineal gland secretes a hormone called melatonin. Light inhibits melatonin secretion and stimulated by darkness. Melatonin secretion is minimal during the day, telling the body that it is not the time for sleep yet. Melatonin secretion is maximal at night telling the body that it is time for sleep.

The internal clock depends on the amount of environmental light to calibrate itself. Other social cues like food, temperature, habits, and routines can also influence the SCN timing, but these are weaker than light.

On an interesting note, all glands in the brain are in pairs except the pineal gland. French philosopher Rene Descartes spend considerable time studying this gland and concluded: "Pineal gland is the central seat of the soul." The pineal gland has fascinated the ancients who called it the third eye. Now we know that the pineal gland can sense light and dark and controls the all-important circadian rhythm by secreting melatonin.

The circadian clock is not functional at birth. Newborns have a free running rhythm, and they can eat, sleep and wake at all times of the day. By three months the 24-hour cycle becomes more regularized to the relief of the new parents. Baby's henceforth stay more wake at day and sleep more at night.

Initially, it was thought that the human clock is around 25 hours and was attributed to the Monday morning blues.

However careful experiments conducted at Harvard University showed that the circadian cycle in human is near to 24 hours like other organisms tuned to the earth's rhythm (of 24 hours). It is slightly higher than 24 hours with a mean of 24.2 hours.

We do not realize this slight difference between our clock and the earth's clock as daily sunlight synchronizes our clock to the earth's. The difference becomes evident in blind people who are insensitive to light. They follow their free-running period of 24.2-hour cycles which after several weeks goes out of sync and they may sleep more at day rather than night.

The ability of the clock to synchronize with light has both advantages and disadvantages. It allows us to get adjusted with the changing light pattern associated with different seasons. The circadian clock performs the best as long as our schedule is aligned with the sun, that is work during the day and rest at night. Whenever we go off these schedules, the circadian clock gets misaligned, and causes sleep problems.

Two specific cases where the circadian clock causes sleep problems are those for night workers and the travelers jet lag. People who work at different hours and especially those working the night shift find it hard to sleep during the daytime after work even if their mind and body is exhausted. Travelers who fly across multiple time zones cannot sleep at the new destination time and suffer from jet lag.

Many of the hormones secreted by the glands of our body follows the circadian clock. Chief among them are Melatonin, Cortisol, Testosterone, Growth hormone and Estrogen. There are however other processes that do not follow circadian rhythm pattern in human like menstrual cycles in females, pregnancy, and lactation-related changes in the female body.

Chapter 13

24.2 HOUR SLEEP CLOCK

In human, the internal clock is 24.2 hours, and these often lead to sleep problems. Many patients complain to me that they do not feel sleepy till 3 or 4 Am, and then struggle to go up and get ready for work. With people working on computer screens, smartphones and tablets- the amount of exposure to artificial light have skyrocketed.

Screen light is disrupting sleep like never before. Let us examine the case of Cloe for better understanding the problem.

Cloe is a 19-year college student with two part-time jobs. After school, she works a few hours at a day care center and a few hours as a waitress on weekends. She is busy but feels happy enjoying her freedom and the extra cash. She wants to go to law school and plans to save some money and pay towards her tuition. Chloe came to me complaining of fatigue, not able to sleep at night, forgetting things, not able to turn up her school work at the time, and staying awake all night and feeling sleepy all day.

On further questioning, she divulged that she hardly gets time to do her school work during the day. After her two jobs, she is finally home by 10 PM, and that's when she starts her school work. She has to write long papers and do research which keeps her awake and glued to the computer screen. In the beginning, she was able to balance her life with classes, jobs and able to finish her assignments and go to bed by 12

AM. She says she doesn't' feel sleepy till 3 to 4 am at night. She hardly sleeps 3 hours, before she has to wake up for her 8 am classes. During the day she feels tired and sleepy. On weekends, she stays up all night working till 6 am on her school projects and then sleeping till noon. She wants to sleep early but can't.

The earth takes 24 hours to complete one rotation on its axis. All life on earth has its internal clock which is wound by this rotation of the earth and follows an approximate 24 hours. So far so good, what about humans? Human also possesses an internal clock with which is around 24.2 hours. Many body processes follow this 24.2-hour periodicity. The clock is readily entrained (calibrated) to the 24-hour cycle through the light entering our retina, stimulating the melanopsin pigment, sending a signal to SCN which is the master clock of the body.

Many of us may wonder well we follow the clock on the wall, on the computer screen and go by the radio and TV hours. You will be amazed to know that, in the absence of all external human-made clocks, out body has its own clock situated in the brain. The clock gets its time cues from the intensity and duration of natural light. Many processes like digestion, sleep, growth, and repair follow a specific timetable. For example, cortisol the primary stress hormone, as well as an activating hormone, is secreted when the body is exposed to light. Melatonin the primary antioxidant hormone as well as a sleep-inducing hormone is secreted only when the body is exposed to darkness. The circadian clock also regulates the secretion of other hormones like sex hormones, growth hormones, and insulin.

The clock of our body is always adjusting to the light exposure. Many tests have been performed where people stayed away from all times cues inside caves, submarines, and underground bunkers. Repeated experiments have shown the body's natural propensity for phase delay and shift to a 24.2 to 25-hour clock in response to unlimited artificial lights.

Subjects given to self-select their sleep and wake times tend to select to go to bed near the fall of their body temperature and tend to rise with the rise in body temperature. The exposure of bright light before bed will activate and energize you, and you will feel sleepy one hour later. Thus, relying on your instincts to sleep when you feel sleepy will put you on a 25-hour cycle. If left unchecked, in a few weeks you will be up all night and sleepy all day. It has been found that when people have access to unlimited light during all 24 hours, they follow a 24.2 to 25-hour cycle. This extra time may look trivial on the surface, but on deep inspection it is sobering.

<u>Let's take the case of Cloe:</u>

On day 1, at her new school, does her schoolwork at night and goes to bed at 11 PM.

On day 2, she does the same amount of work, but don't feel sleepy at 11 pm. She stays awake another hour, checks up on her friends on Facebook, Twitter and then goes to sleep at 12 pm.

On day 3, she does not feel sleepy till 1 AM. She thought about finishing all her work and make use of the time.

On day 4, she does not feel sleepy until 2 am.

On day 5, she does not feel sleepy until 3 am.

On day 6, she is worried, it's 4 am, she still can't sleep. She any-way shuts off the computer, turns off the light and tries to sleep the remaining few hours before she gets up for school at 8 am.

The story sounds familiar! Millions of people around the world are living on a delayed sleep phase due to artificial lights at night. The incandescent lamp of the past used to have light mainly in the yellow and red spectrum which disturbed sleepless. All newer screen devices like computer, laptop, television, smartphone emit a high amount of blue light which blocks the melatonin secretion and causes phase delays to our Circadian clock. Experiments have shown that when the light and dark cues are eliminated, and people have the unrestricted artificial light, they move to a 24.2 to 25-hour cycle. Those with work or family commitments in the morning will struggle to get up unless they have slept early the previous night.

I have seen it taking a full swing and many college students dropping out or switching to online classes. I once saw a student who will stay awake all night till 6 am and sleep till 2 pm. He has to quit college, lost his job and struggled in maintaining relationships. Below is a table showing a hypothetical routine of how only in a manner of ten days, night work with bright light can entirely reverse your sleep cycle with 1-hour phase delay each night.

DAY OF SLEEP	SLEEP TIME
Day 1	Feel sleepy at 9 pm (3 hours after sunset, no artificial light exposure)
Day 2	Watch TV from 6 to 8:30 pm. Feel sleepy at 10 PM.
Day 3	Facebook from 8 to 10 PM. Feels sleepy at 11 PM
Day 4	School work, finish paper from 8 pm to 11 pm. Feels sleepy at 12 PM.
Day 5	Weekend night, party till 12 pm. Feels sleepy at 1 AM.
Day 6	Arranging travel plans and researching on laptop till 12:30 pm. Feels sleepy at 2 am.
Day 7	Exam next day. Study till 2 am. Sleepy at 3 am.
Day 8	Fun time, binge on all Netflix episodes, sleepy at 4 am
Day 9	School at 8 am, can't sleep till 5 am.
Day 10	Staying awake all night, sleeping till noon, feels groggy all day

There is an old saying that "An hour of sleep before midnight is worth two after." Sleep is most efficient when follows the body's natural Circadian rhythm which is in tune with the earth's rhythm. Artificially forwarding the Circadian rhythm using artificial light and sleeping late results in hormonal imbalance and poor sleep quality. Thus, even if someone gets the recommended 9 hours of sleep beginning late, will miss out on the restorative and healing actions of sleep. It's a myth to believe that hours of sleep are all alike like calories from food are all alike. Science has conclusively proven that 100 calories from a gram of spinach are not the same as 100 calories from coke. Similarly, we are slowly learning that timing of sleep is as (if not more) important than total hours of sleep.

Chloe's solution:

Many of us have packed multiple activities in our schedule like Chloe to maximize our opportunities and potential. Here are some general guidelines on how to save sleep even when following a hectic lifestyle

Follow a bedtime routine. Avoid exposure to bright light and computers at least one (better two to three) hour before sleep. Let your eyes get exposed to some darkness. Try to go to bed at the same time.

Bright light exposure at night will push you to a 25-hour cycle. Discipline yourself and try to minimize exposure to light at night. Try to stay at the 24-hour cycle, preferably going to bed not too long after sunset and waking up not too long after sunrise. Reading on the screen tax our eyes the most. We have to stare at the small prints and let all the bright light enter our eyes and send signals to our brain delaying sleep onset.

If you love reading, consider trying audiobooks at night. Some companies are looking for a creative solution. There is a software called flux which I use for my iMac during my nightly work. The software blocks the blue light at night and may minimize some sleep disturbance for those who have to work on screens at night. Blue light from the screen causes maximum sleep disruption. Apple products have an inbuilt night mode which pushes the light through the red spectrum at night. Another option is to use blue light blocking glasses which you can easily order online.

In summary, in this modern age where we spend most time indoors and use artificial lights at night. We can no longer rely on our instincts to go to bed for sleep when we feel sleepy. If we only sleep when we feel sleepy, we will reach a 24.2 to 25-hour cycle and sleep at later hours progressively. Be mindful of your sleep and try to go to bed at the same time to keep your sleep cycle in a 24-hour rhythm.

Chapter 14

SLEEP, ALARM & WAKE TIME

Benjamin Franklin famously said- early to bed, early to rise, makes a man healthy, wealthy and wise. But how early?

Many successful people will swear that they get up at 4 or 5 every day and begin work or work out. Some use an alarm clock to force their body into submission for the early work. In the past, before electricity, most people waked with the sunrise and slept within a few hours of sunset. Getting up at dawn and able to witness the sun is a blessing.

However, there is no health benefit in getting up before the sun. If you are a lark and get up early in the morning after completing 8 hours of sleep- that is Ok. But if you get up first without the 7-8 hours of sleep, there is a problem. If it happens naturally, that means you have a high level of circulating stress hormones which are waking you up. And, if you are using an alarm clock, then you are getting sleep deprived.

Let's go through an everyday morning routine. Lisa gets up at 5.30 with the alarm clock. She takes the dog out for a walk. She wakes up her 5-year-old son John, gets him ready for school. She prepares breakfast for the family. She drops her son to the preschool and drives 30 minutes to reach work by 8 AM. Sounds familiar. Around one-third of Americans is sleep deprived, and the majority has to use an alarm clock to get up and start the day.

The alarm clock has become a life and job saver for many. Now pause for a moment, reflect your morning ritual, and answer truthfully. How many times, did you wake up cursing the alarm clock, putting it into a repeated snooze and eventually woke up grumpy cursing life in general?

Getting up with a morning alarm clock is not optimal for health. The last part of sleep is also the most rejuvenating and waking up should be with peace and ease, and not alarmed. The best way to use an alarm clock is in the evening. Set alarm clock to go to bed. Put an alarm at 8 pm and when it strikes, tell yourself that you have 1 hour more to wrap up everything and hit the bed. You darken your room, go to bed by 9 PM. Your body will take out the required amount of sleep needed and reward you with getting up early morning.

Now based on when you are naturally getting up, you can re-adjust the evening time for alarm. In this way, your body will not be deprived of the rejuvenating sleep, and you will be able to manage all obligations. I got the idea of evening alarm clock from the book by John Durant – 'The Paleo Manifesto: Ancient Wisdom for Lifelong Health' and has used it myself and recommended to my patients with success.

Using an evening alarm clock may sound weird, but it is about training your body. This habit may take time, and like everything, it gets better with practice. In the beginning, I suggest using two alarm clocks- one for the morning and one for the evening. In case your body needs more sleep and refuse to get up, the morning alarm will coax it to do so. Then the next day you set the evening alarm even earlier. You keep on adjusting alarm time, till your body gets up in the morning without the alarm clock.

Most public schools in the United States starts in the morning. Depending on how far one lives, sometimes the school bus will come as early as 6 AM to pick up the children. This is too early for most and disruptive to sleep. Studies have shown that children and teenagers are becoming sleep deprived and it is impairing their ability to learn in school. Also, lack of sleep increases the craving for carbohydrates, sugar, and high-calorie food. Childhood obesity is already a big problem which only gets worse with less sleep. Also, lack of sleep increases the risk for depression, anxiety. Attention disorders and suicidality.

The American Academy of Pediatrics has issued a statement in 2014 that high school and middle schools should not start before 8:30 a.m. Other medical groups have also urged the school boards to delay school and let children sleep more. Some school board has done that which has improved the performance of their students. However, for the majority of schools- it remains a problem.

According to a study by the Rand Corporation in 2017, delaying sleep time to 8.30AM will lead to $9 billion a year in economic gains. The gains happen because later school times will cause a higher academic performance and hence more lifetime earnings. Secondly, money will be saved as well rested teens will drive safer and have fewer car crashes.

As a physician, I am fortunate to have some flexibility of my work schedule. I prefer to start my work at 10 AM. It is late for many, but it allows me to wake up when my body is ready; generally, around 7 am. Then it gives me an hour for exercise, some reading, breakfast. As a bonus, I avoid the peak hour traffic. For many, this is not an option, but try to tweak your schedule to get the most of your sleep.

In summary, remember that the most restful, restorative sleep happens during the end of sleep. You don't want to miss it. Using the morning alarm clock once in a while is OK for emergencies, sudden plan changes or shift work. But otherwise, regular use of alarm clock to wake up will make you sleep deprived in the long run. If you get up with the clock and feel groggy, grumpy, and gauche; your body is telling you then it's not the right time. The solution is to set the alarm in the evening to go to bed early. It will ensure you get adequate sleep and get up refreshed in the morning. Every morning becomes a GOOD MORNING!

Chapter 15

NIGHT & SHIFT WORK

Work is a source of a stressor for many. But when the work has to be done in evening or night, or in swing shift which changes every week- it compounds the stress. Shift work is any work done outside the normal daylight hours of 7 A.M. to 6 P.M. Shift work includes evening and night work, as well as overtime or extra-long workdays. Shift work poses unique challenges to the body and increases the risk of many diseases. Fatigue related to shift work and sleep deprivation has been attributed to industrial disasters like:

1. The nuclear accident at Three Mile Island, Pennsylvania in 1979
2. Chemical accident at the Union Carbide plant in Bhopal, India, in 1984
3. The nuclear accident at Chernobyl in Ukraine in 1986
4. The explosion of the Challenger space shuttle in 1986
5. The Exxon Valdez Oil Spill in Alaska, the USA in 1989

It is estimated that around 20% of workers in industrialized countries are employed in shift work. About 22 million Americans are involved in shift work across various sectors-health, food, retail, transportation, manufacturing, call centers, and public-safety industries like police officers, firefighters, military, and security guards. Shift work poses significant challenges for both the white and blue-collar workers.

Many working in customer care have to cater to people across the globe in different time zones. Many can work from home but have to travel frequently to various cities across time zones causing sleep disruptions. Those employed in the medical sector suffer the most. It affects doctors, nurses, pharmacists who are engaged in shift work to provide round the clock service for patients. Then, there are those employed in gas stations and 24-hour convenience stores working the night shift.

How is shift work injurious to individual health?

Human physiology is the product of millions of years of evolution whereby the norm had humans staying awake during the day and sleeping at night. The modern assault on this sleep-wake cycle also called the circadian rhythm- may have dire health consequences. The hormone melatonin which is produced at night during sleep also happens to be the most potent antioxidant in nature.

When we are awake and exposed to light, melatonin production is suppressed. Research suggests that shift workers' night workers are more likely to sleep less, work more hours, and drive drowsy at least once a month and have poorer overall health when compared with non-shift workers. Shift work, especially night work has been associated with increased risk of cancer, obesity, diabetes, heart disease, digestive problems and menstrual irregularities.

Research has shown the increased link of breast cancer among women working at night. The World Health

Organization has listed shift work disrupting sleep-cycle as a probable carcinogen. Working at night causes disruption with hormones that regulate our hunger and appetite. People staying up late at night will have cravings for sugar and more likely to binge on junk food. A high incidence of obesity and diabetes is thus seen in people who work more at nights. Additionally, shift work increases the risk of developing cluster headaches, heart attacks, sexual dysfunction, depression, dementia, and reproductive disorders. Shift work has also been associated with problems like increased smoking and use of recreational drugs.

Solutions for Shift Workers: For many people, shift work is the only available option. Maintaining healthy sleep hygiene can mitigate some of the dangers. If you are in shift work, try to get as much sleep possible on your rest days. Try to have a nap before and after the shift work. Although caffeine can cause sleep problems in many, it can be beneficial for shift work to increase wakefulness and reduce errors.

Research has shown that shift-workers who take prophylactic naps have reduced errors. There are also medications available which can promote sleep as well as wakefulness. Melatonin is a safe and non-addictive choice, both for short- and long-term use. It helps to restore and increase sleep for night workers. Light inhibits melatonin. It has been seen that blue light causes a maximum reduction in melatonin. Avoidance of bright light (mainly blue) at night improves body's melatonin production.

You can reduce blue light exposure by keeping the room dark, using blue light blocking glasses, and by minimizing the use of TV, computer, laptop, phone, and tablet screens before bedtime. Other medications like stimulants are used to promote wakefulness but not routinely recommended as side effects outweigh the benefits. Similarly, there are sedatives and hypnotics which can improve sleep and work wonders in the short-term for a sleep-deprived person, but their long-term use needs careful oversight by a doctor.

Case Study: John's sleep problem

John is a 35-year-old male. John has recently taken up a new job for better pay to meet the increased expenses of his growing family. John's new post is in a factory, and the only opening position was in graveyard shift (the shift from 12 pm to 8 am). John didn't mind it in the beginning as he could work at night and help with the children at the daytime. However, since joining a few months ago, John had been noticing a decline in his level of energy, concentration, and well-being. He works on the third shift. He can hardly sleep at night and feels tired all the time. He feels miserable, angry and fatigued all the time. And this is getting worse. He fell asleep at his job last night, and the supervisor gave him a warning. He heard from the grapevine that some months back one worker got into a serious accident after dozed off while handling heavy machinery incurring serious injury. John's supervisor suggested changing his schedule to a daily rotation basis to help him out. He had tried that once in a previous job, which made his sleep worse. What can John do to get adequate sleep and rest while still keeping this job?

Sleep Prescription for John

I suggested that John prioritized sleep in his life and discussed it with his family. He will need all the family support, as he has to fight against the natural sleep rhythms of his body, stay alert and be productive at work, and yet be able to wind down and get adequate sleep and rest during the daytime. Many times, doctors fail to incorporate the family into the treatment plan. People live with their families. No matter how perfect the sleep plan unless the family cooperates, it is not going to work. I, therefore, invited the entire family and suggested the following sleep plan-

1. John has to communicate with his supervisor and have a discussion of the current situation. He should make a formal request to be allowed to stay on the same shift for no less than 21 days. Any shift rotation should be made in a clockwise manner. If he works the day-shift for 21 days, then the next shift change will be to an evening-shift, and from the evening-shift to night-shift and finally from night-shift to day-shift. The clockwise shift change will ease the stress of the shift change and allow his body to adjust better.

2. John will take extra care during the evening and night shifts. During his day shift time, he will maintain good sleep hygiene and make sure he is properly rested and should accumulate no sleep debt. He should be fresh and well-rested before the beginning of an evening or night-shift work.

3. During evening shifts which end at 12 PM, he should have a quick dinner as soon as he comes home from work. Avoid all stimulation (TV, the Internet, Phone, Tea, Coffee, Alcohol) post work. Be on the bed as soon as he can. If he

can get good sleep from 2 am to 7, or 8 am, that will be five hours. Any more will not do any harm. A nap in the late afternoon if time allows will keep him more refreshed for the evening shift.

4. Now, the most challenging part is to design the schedule for the night shift work. This is the difficult part where a family help and high self-discipline is needed for success.

Night shift work will begin at 12 am and end at 8 am. When John drives home, he will be getting the daylight which will try to signal his body to stay awake. The light will inhibit melatonin and increase his wakefulness. John needs to minimize this to get sleep at daytime. He can wear sunglasses the following work to decrease the amount of bright light reaching the eyes. It is best to avoid driving after overnight work. When possible, arrange transport through the work or family, if he feels too tired to drive.

Secondly, keep a dark, cold bedroom ready for him. It should be like a dark cave. He has to fool his body to think it is night time. Darkness will stimulate melatonin and inhibit cortisol. Keep the door locked or make sure it's quiet and children don't come and awake him. Arrange help.

John should try to sleep as long as he can, or the situation permits. If necessary, take melatonin tablets, if he can't produce enough melatonin in his body to induce sleepiness. He should try to get a quick nap before he leaves for work at night. If he feels drowsy during the middle of his shift, drinking tea or coffee can be helpful.

He should take the caffeine drinks only at the beginning or the middle of his shift. No caffeine towards the end as it will impair his ability to sleep after the shift finishes at 8 am.

In summary, shift work is disruptive to our sleep and well-being. One has to be careful and take steps to mitigate the sleep disruption caused by shift-work. The science of sleep and shift work has been translated into political action, and safety regulations have now been created for various industries in recognition of the dangers of shift work. The importance of sleep requires more public and personal awareness to increase safety.

Laws and regulations can only go so far. Unless everyone becomes aware of the life-giving property of sleep and makes it a priority, fatigue-related accidents will continue to occur. Additionally, we will continue to see a surge of cancer, obesity, heart disease, diabetes, depression, and other lifestyle illnesses whose incidence can be reduced with improved sleep.

Fortunately, there are ways by which we can reduce the damage caused by shift-work. Use of timely scheduled naps, creating dark rooms during the daytime, avoiding stimulants and other sleep disruptive chemicals, and using over the counter melatonin are some of the remedies. If you do shift work and your sleep and wellbeing remain compromised after all your efforts, consult a doctor. Also, you can contact the National Institute for Occupational Safety and Health at 1-800-35-NIOSH for more information on your rights and options.

Chapter 16

SLEEP DEPRIVATION & DROWSY DRIVING

Sleep can be a matter of life and death. Many people die every year in traffic accidents due to the driver falling asleep behind the wheel. For every 2 hours of wakefulness, we need one hour of sleep. This is biologically driven and a biological requirement. Thus, if we increase the hours of wakefulness without increasing the sleep time, we accumulate sleep debt. The loss of sleep hours will impact the body's performance in wake hours. We can accumulate sleep debt like credit card debt over time.

Ultimately, the body will extract the debt with interest either through forced rest due to illness or by forced sleep during activity. Studies have shown that around 40 percent of the US population is sleep deprived, that amounts to around 120 million people in sleep debt. With so many sleep-deprived people driving daily, drowsy driving has become a major problem in the United States.

Drowsy driving happens when we are sleep deprived over a period of time. Lack of sleep lowers our ability to pay attention to the road. It impairs decision making, and alarmingly, it lowers our reaction time. Thus, drowsy drivers are more prone to miss changes in the road, and struggle to break or steer away due to slower reflexes.

The risk, danger, and tragic results of drowsy driving are alarming. As per national highway traffic safety administration, an estimated 1 in 25 adult drivers (aged 18 years or older) report having fallen asleep while driving in the previous 30 days. Drowsy driving was responsible for 72,000 crashes, 44,000 injuries, and 800 deaths in 2013.

I learned the perils of drowsy driving the hard way. While coming back from a social engagement, I was just 5 miles from my house. Then it happened. I woke up with a loud bang, with the yells and cries of my son and wife. I opened my eyes, and to my horror found myself in car wiggling on a sidewalk. I have dozed off during sleep, and my car swayed away from the road on the pavement for a few seconds, before I wake up to the cry of my wife, mother and my son. I somehow managed to steer the car back on the road. It was 2 AM, on a Saturday night. I was lucky, the road was empty, the sidewalk was empty. Other than some damage to the front of the car, and a flat tire, we were unscathed.

I was lucky. I could have got a severe bodily injury. My wife, my mother, my so--Al that I deeply cared for and lived for, could have been lost. I could have killed some innocent person or hurt someone permanently. I could have been in prison. I could be dead. As I stood on the side road, waiting for the emergency road service to rescues us, I hear my son crying in the car, my wife shaking nervously, and my mother praying. I asked myself, what I did wrong? And how ended up here, now standing just an inch away from death?

2016 was a crucial year for me. I bought my first house. I celebrated my son's first birthday. I was teaching medical students, was doing research, writing books, consulting work, in addition to treating psychiatric patients. it was a time of productivity and creativity. I was making the most money I ever did and accomplishing more than ever. Down the line, I never realized, when I began to neglect my sleep, my nutrition, and exercise. There was always one excuse or the other.

As I began my sleep research, I realized how lucky I was. Every year thousands of Americans die of a car accident as a result of sleeping behind the wheels. I was lucky, but most are not, as road traffic accident carries high fatality in the US. That night was a wakeup call. I made a promise to take my sleep seriously.

While coming back, my mother narrated me the story of a famous Bollywood star Akshay Kumar (Tom Cruise of Bollywood). Akshay is unique in that he makes 4-6 good quality films each year while many similar successful stars could only finish one or two. Here is what he told a newspaper when asked whether he ever compromises on sleep for work. Akshay replied, *"Not at all. I go home on time and usually don't shoot at night unless it is a night sequence. I work only 8 hours a day. I need my full 8 hours sleep and usually sleep by about 10 pm as I get up between 4 and 5 am. And yes, lifestyle is important, so I don't party as I need to get up in the morning. If you start early, you can actually finish half your day's work by 10 am. I have so much time during the day."*

In summary, remember driving is a privilege which comes with great responsibility. Do not drive when you feel sleepy. Stop over, rest, change drivers if available, do not rush, and drive back only when fully alert. Driving when sleepy poses high risks for accidents endangering your life and that of others. Avoid driving late at night after 2 am, because that is the time when we have the maximal urge to sleep. Also, do not drive under influence of alcohol, or any sedating medications. Get enough sleep and follow healthy sleeping habits. Sleep well, drive safe and live longer.

PART IV
SLEEP STRATEGIES

Chapter 17

MINDFULNESS FOR SLEEP

" Sleep is the best meditation."

-Dalai Lama.

In the previous sections, we learned about the science behind sleep and went over the health benefits of sleep. Now let us dive into the lifestyle habits which promotes sound sleep. One may develop sleep problems for various reasons. Fortunately, there are many different sleep strategies that one may apply for good sleep.

Many people have too much activity and thoughts in their mind when they go to bed. An active brain during bedtime impairs the sleep process. One way to calm and still the mind is the practice of mindfulness meditation. The regular practice of mindfulness meditation, even for a short time like ten minutes a day, can help us to be more mindful and reduce stress. Mindfulness is a kind of meditation where one tries to zone in "here and now." One becomes mindful of the present moment. It's living in "here and now" and training the mind to stop dwelling in the past or jumping to the future. Being mindful is the ability to observe and focus on all the internal and external experiences without judgment. It's a practice that can help the mind to focus on the task at hand, rather than running here and there.

The practice of mindfulness is believed to have evolved in the east. Mindfulness has been practiced for many years in Hindu and Buddhist religious traditions. Reference to mindfulness can be found in various Hindu and Buddhist scriptures. Breathing plays an essential role in most of the mindfulness exercises. There are breathing exercises called Pranayama which form an integral part of Hindu Yogic traditions. The word Pranayama originates from a combination of two Sanskrit words, Prana meaning life force and ayāma, to extend or draw out. Pranayama forms the fourth "limb" of the eight limbs of Ashtanga Yoga as explained in verse 2.29 in the Yoga Sutras of Patanjali.

Mindfulness has been practiced in the east for around 3,000 years. Mindfulness was first introduced to the west by Jon Kabat-Zinn, who developed the Mindfulness-based stress reduction (MBSR) program to assist people with diverse medical conditions at the University of Massachusetts Medical Center in 1979. Since then thousands of patients had benefited by the MBSR program. The mindfulness movement has grown immensely and had entered the mainstream. It is being used in schools, prisons, hospitals as well as in law, business, and education. Mindfulness has become part of many psychotherapy programs like Mindfulness-Based Stress Reduction (MBSR), Mindfulness-Based Cognitive Therapy (MBCT), Acceptance and Commitment Therapy (ACT), and Dialectical Behavioral Therapy (DBT). Mindfulness is healthy for the mind, brain and the body.

Physical benefits of mindfulness include improved heart and lung function, regulation of blood pressure, relief of pain and acid reflux, and improved digestion. Psychological benefits of mindfulness include improved sleep, mood, well-being, trauma-recovery; and reduced stress, anxiety, obsession, addiction, and suicidality. Also, mindfulness increases empathy and understanding, of the self and surroundings. It improves satisfaction and makes us happier at whatever we do. It makes us a better – person, spouse, parent, child, sibling, colleague, neighbor and a world citizen.

Mindfulness can be achieved through formal guided practices like meditation or informally by following its principles.

The basic principles of mindfulness can be learned. The essential element is breathing. Breathing is crucial to all body processes. We take our first breath at birth and our last at death. The process of respiration goes on all the time irrespective of our awareness. However, unlike the heart which pumps blood tirelessly, on which we have no voluntary control; we can voluntarily regulate the speed and duration of our breathing cycle. Learning to focus our mind on our breath is an easy way to train our brain to be mindful. Hence breathing regulation is the most common method of various relaxation techniques and mindfulness.

Infants instinctively know the correct way to breath. Infants breathe through the nose, and the belly moves out and in with each breath. Some adults seem to have developed faulty habits related to breathing. Here is a refresher. When one takes air inside one's body, it’s called inspiration. When one exhales air outside, it's called expiration. Nose is the first choice for this air exchange unless one has a medical problem. Mouth breathing has been linked to adenoids, allergy, and asthma. Nose breathing is most efficient and allows maximal air exchange.

A breathing cycle begins with inspiration when the body breathes in the atmospheric air rich in oxygen and uses it for various metabolic processes. The inhaled air after use becomes low in oxygen and high in carbon dioxide. This impure air is exhaled out of the body. The more efficiently the air exchange takes place; the higher amount of oxygen is available to the body. In a calm and relaxed state, one should take slow deep abdominal breaths. The human mind and body are interconnected. The mind can influence the body, and the body can influence the mind. In times of stress and anxiety, our breathing becomes shallow, irregular and faster. During that situation, one can retrain the body into thinking that everything is under control by regulating how you breathe. A slow deep relaxed breathing will send more oxygen to the brain and body and can bring a sense of calmness.

Here is a basic mindfulness exercise called **"Mindfulness-101"** that I teach my patients:

<u>Step 1</u>: Breathing -Inhale as deeply and as slowly as you can and hold it for a split second. Feel your belly bulge with this incoming life-giving air. Then exhale it out through the nose and feel the belly shrink to expel out the air. If you are not sure, put a palm on your abdomen and feel the movement. If you don't feel any motion, then simulate this motion until it becomes a second nature.

<u>Step 2:</u> Counting -The next step is counting. The mind works best when there are a set goal and a time limit. Begin to count each breath and count to 101. Mindfulness- 101 can be done in any posture. Use whatever is comfortable and whatever is available. You can do this while lying flat on a bed or a yoga mat, sitting on a chair, while standing or taking a walk outside. If possible, the outdoor setting is better as you can inhale oxygen-rich fresh air.

This exercise may be practiced once or twice a day. Eyes may remain closed to focus better on the inner experiences; however, Mindfulness- 101 can be done while walking with eyes open. One can take a ten-minute break in the busy day and go for a mindfulness walk or sit down at a quiet place and practice mindfulness-101.

Many thoughts may come during the process, don't worry. Let them come, do not resist, they will go away with their own accord. It's important to focus on the experience and not to analyze or judge. Just observe. Feel any sensation or thought or emotion that may come up. Notice them and let them go. Don't bother to stop and write down any brilliant idea that may come during this period. The thoughts are yours and will be there. You can always write them down at the end. Many have found this process a great tool for brainstorming and problem-solving.

Whenever you feel lost, just put your hand on the belly. Feel rhythmic up and down of your abdomen. Feel the pure, life-giving air, enter your body and fill it with the life-force (also referred to as prana, chi, ki in eastern traditions), and then exit and taking away the toxins out of the body. Many have visualized positive forces entering the body with each breath like peace, serenity, happiness, success, health, vitality and negative forces leaving the body with each exhalation like sorrow, misery, failure, stress, and disease. Some techniques like body-scanning, call for us to focus on different body parts and notice their undulations with each breath. One can use their creativity and imagination and create images suiting their individual needs.

Mindfulness-101 should take around ten minutes. One need

not worry if it takes more or less time. More important is the calming, relaxing and tranquil feeling that one experience afterward. As one done this mindfulness exercise, slowly one builds more stamina for mindfulness meditation. Later, the duration can be increased in the form of repetition of the whole sequence with similar or other images.

One thing needs to be remembered. Mindfulness will not and cannot solve the root cause of the problem. For example, if someone is between jobs, some anxiety is good as it will motivate him to look for another job. However, too much stress can be debilitating, and it can make someone so fearful and hopeless that, so much that he stops searching. Mindfulness can stop the self-defeating thoughts and help one to focus all energies towards a solution which will be re-employment in this case.

There are various mindfulness exercises specifically geared for sleep. There are also mindfulness apps which can be downloaded and used for sleep. Mindfulness helps insomnia in multiple ways.

First, the regular practice of mindfulness synchronizes the brain waves. It helps to make the brain calm and still and prepare it for sleep.

Secondly, mindfulness helps in the secretion of hormone melatonin which is the body's signal for sleep induction.

Thirdly, mindfulness helps to reduce anxiety and depression which can impair sleep.

Fourthly, mindfulness fosters deeper stages of sleep like the dream sleep (REM) and slow wave sleep which are more rejuvenating and restorative.

Compared to medications and therapy, mindfulness is a safer and more comfortable option. It is like riding a bicycle. Once you master the skill, it stays with you for over. There are many organizations which teach mindfulness for free, or with a nominal fee. I have done the happiness course from the Art of Living foundation started by Sri Ravi Shankar. The course focuses on Sudarshan Kriya, a powerful meditation technique with many health benefits.

In summary, mindfulness has multiple health benefits and can be an effective cure for insomnia. Those who are interested in learning more, there is plenty of help available in the form of books, cassettes, videos and guided courses. I highly encourage people to take a live course with a teacher (Guru) who can guide through more advanced stages of mindfulness.

Fortunately, several courses on mindfulness and meditation are available through various groups and organizations. (See resources at the back)

Chapter 18

FOOD FOR SLEEP

People choose their food for religious, spiritual, cultural, communal, and for health reasons. It also depends on the season and availability. Traditional diets all over the world were built around ingredients which were local and readily available. In the beginning, all humans were hunters and gatherers. People foraged wild fruits, berries, and meat of wild animals.

The Last Ice Age also called the Last Glacial Maximum ended around 11,000 years ago. As the glacial ice retreated to the polar caps, this opened up vast acres of land for grains to flourish. The domestication of grains heralded agriculture around 10,000 years ago in the Fertile Crescent (presently Iraq, Syria, Lebanon, Jordan, Israel, and Palestine, Egypt). From there agriculture traveled westwards to Europe and eastwards to Asia around 9000 years ago. Humans have followed a hunter and gatherer lifestyle for 99 percent time of their evolutionary existence on earth, and our metabolism is still adapted to that lifestyle. The lifestyle diseases like obesity, hypertension, diabetes, hypercholesterolemia, insomnia, cancer happens as we follow the sedentary civilized life.

Protein, carbohydrates, and fat constitute the three main foods in our diet. Proteins are the building blocks of life. They are essential for growth and repair. Proteins also act as enzymes, hormones, and neurotransmitters. Protein deficiency can make one tired, sick and stunted.

Recommended Dietary Allowance for protein is 0.8 grams per kg body weight. An adult who weighs 70 kilograms needs at least 56 grams of protein each day. A well-planned diet can supply the required number of proteins using high protein food like milk, meat, beans, nuts, and lentils.

A high carbohydrate diet containing simple sugar will cause blood sugar spikes. When our blood sugar fluctuates, we are more prone to feel stressed. We are tempted to go for comfort food rich in calories and salt. However, the instant high from sugary food gives temporary relief. A diet high in protein, fat, complex carbohydrate will keep the blood sugar stable throughout the day. A nutrient dense diet satisfies bodies need and prevents craving for unhealthy sugary and junk food. It will keep neurotransmitters and hormones work better and help brain handle stress well. Nutrient dense foods are raw or cultured dairy products, cage-free eggs, grass-fed beef, wild-caught fish, poultry, pasture raised chicken, brewer's yeast, organ meat, and green leafy vegetables.

We are what we eat. Eating and drinking is a direct way when our internal environment communicates directly with the external environment. Food influences every aspect of our life from our energy levels, health status, mood changes, disease processes, and sleep patterns. What you eat and when you eat are both critical for sleep. It is advisable not to eat any food for 2 to 3 hours before sleep. Many celebrities and health freaks will not eat anything after sunset, thus giving their body 4 or more hours to digest the last meal before going to bed.

Specific foods have a soothing effect and help to sleep at night, while some foods are more activating and disturb sleep.

Food disrupting sleep:

Caffeine: Food containing caffeine are activating and disturbs sleep. Avoid tea and coffee after 5 pm.

Alcohol: Alcohol helps with sleep. But alcohol-induced sleep tends to be shallow and less rejuvenating as alcohol inhibits the REM sleep.

Sugar: Having sweet desert s part of many culture and celebration. Sugary food before bedtime is unhealthy because it leads to sudden insulin spike and leads to blood sugar fluctuations which disturbs night sleep.

Spicy Food: Fried and spicy food are often difficult to digest. Eating them before bedtime may cause sleep problem due to heartburn and indigestion.

Dark Chocolate: This is controversial as some research funded by chocolate companies show that chocolate before sleep is good. I disagree. Dark chocolate contains sugar and caffeine. Both are too stimulating for sleep. Organic dark chocolate contains polyphenols rich in antioxidants which have many health benefits. Have your desserts including dark chocolate or red wine a few hours before bedtime so that they do not disturb sleep.

Junk Food: Try to avoid junk food at night. In the morning we are busy, and we worked during lunch and had to resort to fast food. That's Ok. But try to have a healthy meal at night. Junk food consisting of refined sugar, processed fat, white bread, white pasta will cause weight gain and increased blood cholesterol. Avoid eating them at night as the body has less time to burn those calories.

Food Promoting Sleep:

Complex carbohydrates: Brown rice, brown bread, oats, whole grains retain their nutrients and are a healthier option. They boost the serotonin levels and are activate the parasympathetic system promoting sleep.

Nuts: Almonds, cashews, pistachios, walnuts, pecans are all good snack choices before sleep. Nuts are rich in magnesium which has a calming effect on the brain. Try to avoid deep fried nuts. Choose raw nuts, soaked nuts, and even better-sprouted nuts. Although more work, the best way to consume nuts is to buy organic, then soak them overnight, rinse the water, let them sprout, then dry them, and finally bake them.

Herbal Tea: This should not be confused with regular tea which is rich in caffeine. A nightly cup of herbal tea can be a perfect relaxing sleep ritual before bed. When shopping, look for herbal tea containing chamomile, ginger, or peppermint.

Fruits: For those with a sweet tooth, fruits are a good substitute for sweet dessert. Choose local, seasonal, ripe fruits. Bananas are useful in particular because they are rich in tryptophan. Other good choices are papaya, pineapple, mango, kiwi, and berries. But do not overdo as fruits are also high in water and sugar.

Warm Milk: In India, it is common to drink a cup of warm milk with almond or cashew before bedtime. Warm whole milk in high in good fat and tryptophan which promotes sleep.

Eggs & Red Meat: Meat products are high in tryptophan

and saturated fat. Most people associate tryptophan as something present in turkey which makes us sleepy after the Thanksgiving meals. However, tryptophan is present in all red meat products as well as in milk and egg yolks. Tryptophan gets converted to serotonin and melatonin in the body which promotes sleep.

Be careful about where you get your animal products. Fat stores nutrients and toxins. Fat from animal given antibiotics, hormones, genetically modified corn, confined in cages will become unhealthy. However, the same fat from organic cage free pastured animals will be high in vitamins and nutrients. Meat from healthy animals will be healthy for human consumption and help with the sleep process.

Chapter 19

FOOD FOR WEIGHT LOSS

Overweight people are at increased risk for sleep problems like Obstructive Sleep Apnea. I have discussed Sleep Apnea in detail at a later section. Food plays a significant role in weight control. Specific food is notorious for causing weight gain and obesity. Although too much focus is put on the fat and the calorie content of the food, the real culprits are the processed and refined food. In earlier times, people used to eat fresh fruits, fresh vegetables, and fresh meat. Now most of us buy our food from the big grocery stores like Wal-Mart, Costco, Kroger, and Publix.

We enjoy the convenience to get the food when we want and what we want. But this shift from eating fresh and seasonal has consequences. All natural and whole foods are nutrient dense rich in vitamins, minerals, and antioxidants. During the processing, many nutrients are lost. Natural food is rich in potassium and low in sodium, but when preserved and processed this ratio is altered. The processed food is high is in sodium, and low in potassium. The nutrient level is at its peak when the fruit or vegetable is plucked from the tree, and for meat at its source. But as the food stays in cold storage, it loses nutrients over time. Here are the four common food ingredients of concern:

Food causing weight gain

Sugar: Americans are fond of sweets. All events and celebrations are marked by sweets. All candies, coke, drinks, donuts come are artificially sweetened. Sugar is bad for health and causes weight gain, diabetes, tooth damage, and host of other problems. However, sugar is not the worst. Most sweets in the US are made of high fructose corn syrup which is chemically processed and has deleterious health consequences. The corn syrup is kept artificially cheaper in the US by the farm subsidies. As a result, all the sugary beverages high in calories like coke, cookies, candies, chocolates, cakes are cheaper and readily available. These have empty calories and last longer- both outside and inside the body. They are also less expensive than products made of cane sugar. They are everywhere, and form an integral part of the American culture, and are hard to resist.

High fructose corn syrup has been directly linked to metabolic syndrome which is a condition where the blood pressure, blood sugar, blood cholesterol, blood triglycerides, and the waist circumference goes up leading directly to obesity. Hence, make every possible attempt to eliminate sugar and corn syrup from your diet. Try natural sweetener like honey and maple syrup instead. Stay away from zero calorie drinks which contain aspartame. In the long run, they cause more weight gain and a host of metabolic problems.

Wheat: Wheat is an integral part of the civilized diet. It is a staple food and present in the cereals, noodles, pasta, bagels, muffins, pancakes, waffles, donuts, pretzels, crackers. Escaping wheat in America is hard. Wheat was first domesticated around 8000 years ago in the Fertile Crescent and had been consumed since then. Wheat was successfully harvested, eaten and digested by our forefathers in a healthy way. Now one may ask- what's wrong with the wheat which was good for our grandparents and great-grandparents? The wheat we eat now is not the same wheat used by our grandparents.

The current strain of the wheat is a product of genetic engineering. The high yielding wheat- Triticum Aestivum, has now replaced the older sturdy ones, and are now cultivated across the world. This modern wheat, also called the common wheat, constitutes 95 percent of all wheat grown in the world. It has much higher gluten content, and as a result, we now see a rise of gluten sensitivity and celiac diseases. The modern wheat has fewer nutrients and more starch. It increases the blood sugar more rapidly. It tends to store in the body more readily and causes obesity. Also, the modern wheat made by genetic engineering is too fragile to survive on its own and requires massive doses of pesticides and artificial fertilizers. Try to limit the amount of wheat in the diet, or replace them with oats, quinoa, and wild rice.

Potato: Potatoes are ubiquitous in America. They are in virtually in all dishes from stocks, soups, and fries. Historically, potatoes were first introduced to Europe and Asia by the Spaniards and the Portuguese who brought them from the Americas around 500 years ago. Potatoes are a nutritious food, and the Native Americans consumed them in abundance.

But the way, most potatoes are cooked today, it causes obesity. The French fries are potatoes deep fried. It generates trans-fatty acid which is detrimental to health. The frying process eliminates most of the nutrients, and also increases the glycemic index of potato. High glycemic index means it will raise the blood sugar rapidly, and this contributes to diabetes and obesity. Since potato is easy to grow, store and cook, it has been historically replacing other nutritious vegetables from the daily menu. Thus, limiting potatoes in the diet and replacing them with other vegetables like carrot, beet, squash, and papaya will help lose weight.

Refined vegetable oils: Vegetable oils are a relatively new food in our diet. They were nonexistent before 1900. These are industrially prepared by extracting oil from the seeds of rapeseed, soybean, corn, sunflower, sunflower, safflower, cottonseed, and rice bran oil. They are one of the most chemically altered foods in our diet. They are found in all processed food.

Vegetable oils are high in trans fatty acids which causes cardiovascular diseases. These oils are rich in omega 6 fatty acids. They alter the balance between omega 6 and omega 3 in the body and make the body more prone to inflammation. Excess Omega 6 can cause arthritis, allergy, pain, and disrupt heart and brain function. Choose healthier and more traditional oil that has been in use of thousand years like coconut, palm, and olive oil. Butter, ghee, and lard are a good alternative.

Fat: Many people are afraid of eating fats for health reasons and obesity. The truth is not straightforward. Fat serves multiple functions in the body. One is producing the hormones and neurotransmitters. Second, they are also a storage organ for nutrients and even for toxins. Thus, fat from a healthy pasture raised animal will be high in omega 3, vitamin D, A, K, E and other nutrients.

Similarly, fat from an industrial animal will be rich in antibiotics, pesticides and other toxins the animal is exposed while growing up in the concentrated animal feeding operation. Most research that showed fat as an unhealthy food choice was done using animals raised in the inhumane condition without access to sunlight, fresh air, and grass. Human has been eating fat throughout history. They are the prized parts of the primitive cultures that enjoyed robust health. Secondly, the fat in the blood comes mainly from the carbohydrates and sugar in the diet, and less from the fat we eat.

Elevated fat in the blood is unhealthy as conditions like hypercholesterolemia, and hypertriglyceridemia increases the risk of stroke and heart attack. Majority of the fat in the blood comes from the sugar and simple carbohydrates like bread, pasta, candy, donut, cookie, rice, potato, muffins. These have a high glycemic index, and they cause the blood sugar to go up, creating an insulin spike. The insulin converts excess sugar into fat in the liver and then releases them in the blood to be stored in various organs. Over time, more carbohydrates we eat, more fat we accumulate. At some point, organs become resistant to insulin, and we develop diabetes and other metabolic syndromes.

We need some saturated fat in our diet to stay healthy. Our brain, nerves, skin, eyes, hormones, neurotransmitters, organs- all contain saturated fat, and they require the saturated fat in our diet for normal functioning. So, make sure to take adequate saturated fat in your diet. Make sure the fat comes from a healthy source and check the labels.

In summary, choose your food wisely. Food can heal, food can harm. Find out the local farmers' market around your house. Getting fresh ingredients which are locally, and seasonally directly from the farmers will ensure you get the fresh quality produce at their peak nutritional value. They are a little expensive compared to big retailers like Walmart, Kroger, and Publix. But in the long run, you save much more from the health benefits. However, we lead busy lives. Many times, we do not have time to search and find a local market. Many big retail stores are now keeping organic products. The price of organic food has come down in the last few years as awareness is increasing. If you can afford, always choose organic as, by law, they are free from, additives and preservatives.

Chapter 20

STRESS MANAGEMENT FOR SLEEP

When are under stress, there is an elevation of stress hormones, also called cortisol in your blood. The stress hormones activate us and prepare us for the fight and flight essential for survival. The stress response is useful if you are running away from a war zone or surviving a hurricane. But on a daily basis chronic stress disturbs sleep. There is always some reason for stress. Unless the problem is solved, stress will linger. However, when stress is a result of trauma or severe life problem, it is better to seek professional guidance to identify and manage the stressors. A detailed discussion of stress management can be found in my other book titled Stress rescue.

Healthy diet, adequate sleep, and exercise builds up immunity and helps us to cope with stress better. Sleep and stress are interrelated. Lack of sleep causes stress and raises the stress hormones like cortisol. Vice versa, chronic stress leads to elevated cortisol which impairs our ability to relax and fall asleep at night. Here are some lifestyle changes that help reducing stress management.

The power of good habit: Human are creatures of habit. Aristotle said- "We are what we repeatedly do. Excellence is not an act, but a habit." Regulate your life by having predictable habit patterns. It takes around 60 days of the repeated act to form a new habit. Making lifestyle changes is not easy. Use the power of habit to make these tasks seamless. Besides, you can significantly enhance your productivity by having set times for going to bed, getting up, eating breakfast, lunch, and dinner, moving your bowels, etc. Most successful and happy people have well-regulated lives.

Give up bad habits: If you are a smoker, quit smoking. Smoking is the worst thing you can do to your body and your relationships with others. Stay away from street drugs. They will ruin your physical and mental health in no time. If you are an alcoholic, take charge of it before it destroys your life. Get help, join alcoholics anonymous, and get rehab if needed. You can drink alcohol in moderation. A glass of red wine before meals might even be good for your heart if you are not taking other drugs.

Pick up a Hobby: Children get bored quickly. They are always playing and exploring their environment. But for adults, to make a living, we have to gain expertise in a particular field. As we grow up, we became specialized and performed the same task repeatedly. The brain also craves variety and novelty. One way to counter boredom is to try a pick up a new hobby. Choose something for fun. You may never become great or famous, but who cares. Not everything one does has to generate money. As long as it makes you happy, that's all matters. Choose something easy to do at first which you can afford time and money wise. Ideally, it should be something different from your work. If you are a white-collar worker sitting at your desk all day, then choose a hobby which will make you move more. Gardening, playing a musical instrument, outdoor sports are good options.

Avoid Multitasking: The human brain cannot multitask. When we multitask, the brain shifts from one task to the other. It always does one job at a time. In the long run, multitasking lowers productivity and causes stress. The constant on and off, and shift from one task to the other-tires the brain quickly compared to doing one work at a time. Multitasking can endanger life. Texting and driving cause traffic accidents. Have a scheduled time for your activities. Checking social media inputs on your smartphone every hour while at work or at home is bad for work and the family. Schedule time for email, Facebook, and other obligations. Once you do one thing at a time, you will be amazed at the increased level of energy, relaxation, and productivity that will ensue.

Be Social: When we are relaxing with friends and family, our stress level drops. Paradoxically when we are among strangers, or at professional work place-we have to keep our guard. Too much time at work or among strangers is stressful. Make sure to spend time at home with family. Catch up with your old friends. Connect with people who are positive for you. Avoid groups where you are belittled. If you are the one- declining social invitations for work, keep a separate chunk of time in your calendar for socialization. Lonely people succumb more easily to stress. People with a strong social network deal with stress much better. Also, in most complex problems two brains are better than one. When we have people to discuss your concerns, you gain different perspectives and come out with better solutions.

Donate & Volunteer: Americans are known for their charitable and volunteering activities. The US citizens make maximum donations for all causes across the world. When we give our time and money for noble causes, we feel good about ourselves. If we always think of our selfish needs, we become unhappy and stressed. The only way to combat greed and selfishness is to do charity. And these are the perfect places to meet new positive people and make friends. As everyone is working for a bigger cause, people are more trusting and less judgmental. We feel good about ourselves when we make a positive impact on others. It boosts self-esteem. And these are the perfect platform to hone your leadership, managerial, and organizational skills.

Bibliotherapy: Reading books can reduce stress and improve mental health. There is a long tradition of reading to gain insight and understanding for healing purposes. The term bibliotherapy means therapeutic reading. When we read, our mind expands with new ideas, thoughts, and feelings. We can have a shared understanding of events through reading which we never encountered. We can heal our problems by reading and gaining insights. Many successful people learn the tricks of money, time and people management from their parents or mentors while growing up. If you missed out, you could still catch up by learning life skills through reading. Reading fiction helps us to understand other people as we look at the world from the perspective of different characters. We learn about different motivations and psychology. Reading history broadens our outlook and gives us the proper perspective. By reading a biography, you will have access to the great minds of the world. You can learn how people have faced problems similar to yours and triumphed.

Have a Pet: Many people for various reasons find themselves lonely. For them, the next best thing is to have a pet. Pet owners experience a lower level of stress for multiple reasons. Pets like dogs provide unconditional love. You can cuddle your pet and get the therapeutic touch. You have to take them for a walk every day. Caring for a pet will force you to slow down, go outdoors and get exercise. Having a pet may lower your anxiety levels and depression. Veterans suffering from post-traumatic stress do well when given a therapeutic pet dog.

Keep a Gratitude Diary: When our chips are down, the mind tends to focus on the negative. We lose track of the good things we have and only lament what we don't. Maintain a list of things that you are is grateful for. Count your blessings. List all things going well for you in life. List the things that you are fortunate about. On an average, the incidents of good luck and bad luck should even out. When you feel sad, unlucky, and dejected, going through the gratitude diary can put you in the right perspective. Make it a habit of expressing your gratitude about the positives in your life either through writing or speaking about them.

Music: Listen to your favorite music can make you feel relaxed and provide temporary relief from stress. Classical music can calm the mind. Many use background music in their work to feel calm. Singing or playing a musical instrument is even better. Playing music has shown to improve brain function. Teaching children music early on can also increase their IQ.

Take Vacation: Americans work more extended hours and take the least number of vacations compared to other developed nations. It's crucial to take days off from work and relax. Make sure to use all your leave days. Holiday with loved ones helps you create happy memories. Do not take any job-related work with you while on vacation. Send an email to all-notifying the days you will be unavailable, and the person responsible for your work. The brain needs complete relaxation. You will be surprised at your increased productivity and creativity on return. Additionally, in times of distress, looking at those happy holiday pictures will make you smile.

Be a part of the Group: Be a part of the group based on your inclinations. If you are of a religious type, attend your church, mosque or temple group. Attend regular prayers; participate in the choirs, Volunteer at Sunday schools. Remain involved. If you feel strongly about the environment, join groups like Sierra Club. There are groups for every theme imaginable ranging from science, history, excursion, hiking, running. In addition to socialization, you will be able to interact with like-minded people. You will be able to make friends and vent out share feelings. Ideally, the groups should be nonprofit and should not turn into a second job.

Physical intimacy: Physical touch has healing benefits. The feel of loved ones lowers our stress hormone along with reducing blood pressure and heart rates. Kissing cuddling, hugging, making love all are natural stress busters. Couples who touch each other more experience a lower level of stress. Animal studies have shown that babies who were touched by their mothers grew up more stress resilient as an adult. Married people and couples living together experience a lower level of stress. Lack of affectionate touch may be a reason why single and loners die early.

Massage: Massage is another form of touch where a masseur will press, rub, and manipulate the skin, muscles, and tendons of the body. Massage feels good. Massage is good for muscle sore, back pain, headache and other bodily pain. Massage can lower stress in various ways. Massage increases blood circulation in the body. It also stimulates the lymphatic flow which enhances immunity. Massage also releases endorphins which are the natural painkillers of the body. Massages come in various forms -Swedish massage, Deep massage, Trigger point massage. Try different ones and see which ones work for you.

Minimize Commute: Americans are fond of cars. After the Second World War, the presence of cheap oil, affordable cars, and abundant land gave rise to the suburban culture. In most cities now, people spend around one hour for their commute. In rush hours commute time can easily exceed two to three hours a day. Spending time in a commute can raise blood pressure, blood sugar, blood cholesterol levels. Prolonged sitting in the car also causes back pain, shoulder, and neck pain. Commute also increases our stress levels. It decreases our happiness and life satisfaction. Try to live as close to the job. Plan your travel in advance, so that you spend less time behind the wheels.

Supplements: I am not a big fan of supplements. All the nutrients should ideally be obtained from food. However, it is not always possible. Due to political reasons like farm subsidies, fresh food is more expensive than processed food in the US. Thus, for many, supplements become an economical and practical approach.

Certain natural supplements can complement the nutrients in your diet. There is limited evidence on the use of supplements since the federal drug administration does not regulate them. Use them only after consulting a naturopath or someone qualified in complementary medicine. Here are a few points. Aromatherapy using essential oils such as lavender, myrrh, frankincense, and bergamot can also help you feel calm, and reduce inflammation and stress.

If the stress causes sleep problems, then try melatonin, magnesium, and valerian root. If stress symptoms cause fatigue- try Rhodiola, Ashwagandha (Indian Ginseng). If stress causes poor immunity, then try vitamin C, vitamin b complex, Astragalus. If stress causes bodily pain- try curcumin, omega 3 and vitamin D. If stress causes anxiety and depression- try St-John's Wort. Remember always take supplements in consultation with your doctor as they can react with the medications that you are already taking.

Spend Time Outdoors: We are now staying most of our time indoors which is a significant shift from the past. Time spend in outdoors among nature has multiple health benefits. We have access to fresh air full of oxygen and healthy microbes. We get sun exposure which helps the body to make natural vitamin D. Low vitamin D levels in the blood have been correlated with hypertension. Thus, sun exposure in moderation will boost the vitamin D levels in the body and help lower the blood pressure. Spending time outdoors also raise the endorphin levels which makes us feel good and decreases the stress hormones. Morning and evening walks are ideal with friends and family. If not, get a pet, it will force you to spend some outdoors.

Control your weight: Obesity is a significant risk factor for multiple medical conditions like diabetes, hypertension stroke; as well as mental problems like stress and depression. As we age, we become sedentary and gain weight. The more body mass we have, the harder the heart has to pump the blood across the body. Losing the weight will improve mood and give a more positive outlook on life. However, losing weight is not easy and will require high levels of commitment towards healthy lifestyle choices. Proper diet, good sleep, proper exercise will reduce weight and improve sleep, which in turn will keep the spirits high and build resilience.

Practice moderation: As we get old, our bodies begin to show signs of wear and tear. Aches and pains become common. Body's ability to fight stress goes down. Health problem begins to emerge. Stressed people, many times resort to unhealthy coping ways like overeating, smoking, excessive drinking, drug abuse and reckless sexual activity. Most people who indulge in these excesses come down with numerous physical illnesses as they get old. Many become disabled on account of heart disease, lung disease, liver and stomach disease, bone and joint disease, diabetes, and the like. These health problems take away one's peace of mind, enjoyment and financial security.

Managing one's health requires moderation. Even good habits done in excess can backfire. Often people can get so much into one healthy habit that they fail to meet the basic needs of the body. These are adequate rest, nutrition, timely meals, nutrients, regularity in bowel movements and exercise. Often, people are too busy making money that they fail to meet these requirements of the body. Also, make sure not to overdo it. Many people become obsessed with exercise and diet to the point of becoming antisocial. Some over-exercise while restricting calories and develop eating disorders. Most religions extoll the virtue of moderation, and this guidance will serve humanity for good.

Chapter 21

EXERCISE FOR SLEEP

Sleep is a million-dollar industry. The system churns out thousands of sleep specialists, along with sleep medications, gazettes, and gizmos every year. Also, there are a plethora of supplements- both synthetic, and natural, animal-based and herbal. All of them play an important role and are explained in subsequent chapters. But all this are ancillary. Of everything, you will learn in this book, remember that the number-one aid for sleep is exercise.

A sedentary lifestyle is a major cause of sleep problems. People who engage in hard physical labor and those who exercise regularly sleep better. Exercise has multiple health benefits. It decreases the risks of cardiovascular diseases, diabetes, hypertension, stroke, cancer, depression and anxiety. There is a vast amount of data linking a physically active lifestyle to lower rates of morbidity and mortality. All the body functions benefits from exercise. Exercise even stimulates the formation of new neurons in the brain by activating brain growth factors. From maximum benefit, exercise needs to be done on a regular basis.

Choose the form of exercise you may enjoy like running, walking, swimming, dancing, soccer, tennis, etc. As long as you experience physical exertion, you will reap the benefit. Those with less time can try high-intensity exercises like sprints. It is better to do exercise in a group as people can motivate and inspire each other. The popularity of group fitness classes like Crossfit and Orangetheory fitness is a testimonial to this.

According to the US Department of Health and Human Services - "Some physical activity is better than none. Inactive adults should gradually increase their level of activity. People gain health benefits from as little as 60 minutes of moderate-intensity aerobic activity per week. For major health benefits, do at least 150 minutes of moderate-intensity aerobic activity or 75 minutes of vigorous-intensity aerobic activity each week. Another option is to do a combination of both. A general rule is that 2 minutes of moderate-intensity activity counts the same as 1 minute of vigorous-intensity activity. For even more health benefits, do 300 minutes of moderate-intensity aerobic activity or 150 minutes of vigorous-intensity activity each week or a combination of both.

The more active you are, the more you will benefit. When doing aerobic activity, do it for at least 10 minutes at a time. Spread the activity throughout the week. Muscle-strengthening activities that are moderate or vigorous intensity should be included 2 or more days a week. These activities should work all of the major muscle groups -legs, hips, back, chest, abdomen, shoulders, and arms. Examples include lifting weights, working with resistance bands, and doing sit-ups and pushups, yoga, and heavy gardening."

However, as most of the work we do uses machine power, this may not be even enough. For sedentary workers, there is bad news. New research reveals that one hour of activity is not enough to mitigate the harms of 23 hours of inactivity. This new finding is revolutionizing how we think about exercise.

The human body is a product of millions of years of evolution. It was never meant to be sedentary. If you are an average Indian American, your usual day begins with sitting at the table eating your breakfast, then sitting in your car or a bus or train going to work. At work, you will sit at your desk for eight hours and then return home while sitting in a motorized vehicle. You will have dinner while sitting, and then watch TV while relaxing on a couch. Some of you may go for a run or lift weights for an hour in the gym. In total, the average Indian American is sitting more than 9 hours a day. This excess sitting is an all-time high in recorded history.

The association between sitting and mortality is dose dependent; the more you sit, the less you live. The reduced lifespan due to sitting does not depend on your body weight or exercise time. It means that no matter how much exercise we get, how healthy we eat, how slim we remain, the dangers of prolonged sitting will still cause harm. Nothing can counteract the detrimental effects of prolonged inactivity. Sitting shortens lifespan. Sitting is as harmful as smoking cigarettes and can be considered a disease like smoking. Studies have shown that even four hours of sitting will change your body's metabolism. Sitting is especially harmful to women. Women who sit for more than 6 hours per day have a 40 percent increased all-cause death rate compared to those sitting less than 3 hours per day! This association is not affected by the amount of physical activity women receive.

If we look back in history until very recent times, humans have always been moving. In the beginning, we were all hunter and gatherers. We used to forage for food. Then the economy switched to pastoral and later full time agricultural. At that time most people worked on farms with limited machinery and no electricity. Human and animal labor accomplished all work at home and outside. After the industrial revolution, things began to change as fossil fuels and electricity replaced physical labor. Now we are at the end. In this digital age, almost everything can be done seated. Although tools and technology changed our environment, our body has not had time to evolve. Scientists and anthropologists conclude that the human body has not changed much over the last 40,000 years.

Now, the challenge becomes how to create circumstances where we can coax our bodies to move when it serves no additional benefit. Humans are purposeful animals. That is why it is so difficult for us to motivate ourselves to eat healthily and exercise more. But does this mean that we are all doomed to sit on our buttocks and die early? Is there any hope? Well, humans are also ingenious and problem solvers by nature. As the old cliché goes, necessity is the mother of invention. We see that the market has responded with many creative fitness gadgets to motivate us to move and make it easier to exercise.

One such innovation is the Standing Desk, which makes you stand and work, and the Treadmill Desk, which makes you walk and work. As companies are becoming aware of the cost of sitting and the sedentary life, some are offering standing and treadmill desks for their employees. Many stylish products are available in the market from Lifespan, NordicTrack, Exerpeutic and more. Another useful device is the wearable fitness tracker which measures heart rate, steps, miles walked, sleep hours, and hours of activity and inactivity. There are many choices in all styles and prices from Jawbone, Fitbit, Garmin, Apple and Samsung watches.

Some of the products available today are very expensive, but prices are becoming more affordable as the market expands. There are even inexpensive DIY options. You can make a workable standing desk using a box or stool over the regular desk. A spare treadmill or standing cycle can be placed under the desk. And pedometer smartphone apps are available that, although less accurate, will record all steps and movements of the day.

As a practicing Indian American psychiatrist, I had to spend a lot of time sitting and listening to people's stories and then documenting them. As I got busy in my practice, I began to develop back and neck pain from prolonged sitting. And there was weight gain, despite my eating healthy and exercising regularly. It made me rethink the way I structure my day. I made changes to my schedule. I placed a small table on top of my desk and converted it into a standing desk. I try to do all my reading, typing and writing while standing. When I get tired I'll sit down and take rest, then I will stand again and continue. Some of my coworkers have seen me doing that, and they have also put a small platform over their desk in order to use the computer keyboard while standing. Many of us suffer from back pain, neck pain, and wrist pain. Many people, including myself, have seen these pains go away once their posture is changed from sitting to standing.

I strongly encourage everyone to have a standing desk or make one. While you are working, get up and move every 15 minutes. Use a pedometer or a fitness tracker. A mundane and boring activity like walking and moving can become fun and competitive once you measure and compare with family and friends. I wear a Fitbit Charge and try to do the recommended 10,000 steps per day. There are small lifestyle changes you can also make. Park your car a little further, so that you are forced to walk. Run as many errands as possible by walking. Walk and talk instead of texting or emailing when you can. Stand while you talk on the phone. Prefer to speak with the person face-to-face rather than texting them. Seek all opportunities to move. Some offices are holding standing and walking meetings. People are surprised how things speed up when we move. Lastly, I got rid of the copier and printer from my office. It has freed up my office space and also forced me to walk down the hallway to get papers. I stopped bringing bottled water and now use a recyclable mug. Every time I get thirsty, I walk to the common area to refill my water. In addition to moving, it allows a chance to share ideas with your colleagues and catch up with the latest gossip.

In 2016, I was holding three jobs at a time, and was working all seven days a week and was taking calls two nights a week. I was sleep deprived. I was exercise deprived. I was relaxation deprived. But I had money at my disposal. I bought expensive food and even hired a part-time cook. I was going to the gym but was too tired to exert fully. I could not sleep. My body was mentally tired but physically unfatigued. I was getting up at early mornings around 4 am and could not go back to sleep. My residual stress hormone cortisol level was chronically higher. That was also the time I once fell asleep while driving, as I discussed in the chapter- Sleep and driving.

I knew that exercise, sleep, and nutrition are the keys to health. Of them, sleep is the most crucial. But you cannot just fall asleep. The most healing phase of sleep, the deep stages, is triggered by physical activity and exercise. If you do not exercise, you may still fall asleep, using various other things, but the deep sleep will be missing. In my journey back to health, I reduced my workload, eliminated unnecessary stress- I allowed my body to sleep as much it wants.

But I still could not sleep. I tried all, but my sleep was still 5-6 hours per night. Then I increased my exercise level. I postponed my work day to 10 AM. I started going to the gym and lift weights in the morning. In the evening, I started playing sports like badminton, tennis, cricket for 1 hour. The evening one was more relaxing, and for fun and socializing. But, not socializing like watching a movie, or eating out. It involved physical activity.

Lo & behold, I was sleeping like a baby 8 to 9 hour every night. I remember, the Memorial Day weekend, I went to the Lake Lanier resorts with my family and friends. It was beautiful with the brown hills, green meadows, and the blue water, with the sunbathing them. I hiked about a mile and then swam in the water for 2 hours. When I came back at 7 pm, I was dog tired. I had a light meal and hit the bed. The lights were no, there were sounds, but I was unperturbed. Generally, I cannot sleep with these distractions, but that night, I slept and slept for ten straight hours.

In conclusion, the quickest and the most effective way to get your sleep back is to bump up your exercise schedule. Based on your conditioning, you have to determine the quantity and quality of physical activity to make you tired. Walking 1 hour every evening after dinner is a good way to check the process. If you don't get tired, then carry some weights like a dumbbell or wear a weighted vest.

Slowly, and steadily, keep on increasing the exercise load, until you get sound sleep. For people with a busy schedule, I recommend, exercising twice daily. 15 minutes to 1 hour in the morning, and around half an hour to 1 hour in the evening. Parents with small children often struggle to find time for exercise. One solution is to get a treadmill in the living room. Many errands like watching television or talking over the phone can be done while walking on the treadmill. You can even install a treadmill desk to work on computers and laptops while walking on the treadmill. Use your creativity and determination, as when there is will there is a way. When I just had my baby, I used to carry him in my lap and go on for walks. It was a good exercise for me, and it soothed the baby. Remember, sleep at night is the reward for a day well exercised.

Chapter 22

BEST LIGHT FOR WORK AND SLEEP

We are all aware of junk food (like coke, burger, fries, nuggets) and their dangers. Junk food gives us excess calories without providing the nutrition. But few are aware of the risks of Junk light. Junk light is the artificial light coming from fluorescent, LED, and the screens of the computer, laptop, and smartphones. Junk light emits excess blue light and no infrared and ultraviolet rays. Junk food gives us malnourishment.

Similarly, junk light gives us malillumination, a term coined by Dr. John Ott. In the past, most of our light came either from the sun or through fire generated by burning wood, coal, fat and oil. Then at the beginning of the 19th century, Edison invented the incandescent light. Fire and incandescent light are closer to natural light as they give more natural light rays.

However, the old lights, consumed too much energy as they gave out the infrared light along with red, orange, and yellow lights. In recent years there is a big shift to replace all old lights with the new energy efficient Compact fluorescents (CFLs) and LEDs. These are energy efficient because they only emit waves which we can see and omit the infra-red and the ultraviolet.

Natural light coming from the sun is full spectrum light which contains the seven wavelengths of the visible spectrum along with other electromagnetic waves like infrared, and ultraviolet which our eyes cannot see, but our body feels.

Junk light, on the contrary, is limited to a narrow spectrum and are blue light dominant. Among the visual spectrum, blue lights have the shortest wavelength and the highest frequency. Blue has the highest energy and maximum penetrating power. Artificial lights have five times more blue waves than the sunlight.

The increased amount of blue light comes at the expense of the infrared light, and the ultraviolet light. Although our eyes cannot use them for vision, our body needs them. The infrared light is felt by the body as heat and is required for mitochondrial function and are excellent for detoxification. The ultraviolet rays are used by our skin to make vitamin D and endorphins. In addition, light regulates the release of hormones like testosterone, growth hormone, cortisol and neurotransmitters like serotonin, dopamine, and melatonin. All these determine our mood, energy, motivation, health, and happiness.

Common Problems with Junk light:

Eye Strain & Exhaustion: Artificial bright light causes pupillary constriction. Then reading on the computer forces our eyes to focus closer. Prolonged use causes eye strain and increases the risk of nearsightedness or myopia. Also, the brain spends an enormous amount of energy to process the visual stimuli. Of all lights, blue requires the maximum energy and can overhaul the visual cortex, causing exhaustion. I first became aware of this when my medical practice switched from paper charts and to electronic health records. I saw the same number of patients, did the same documentation, and provided the same clinical care. But at the end of the workday, I felt more tired. Later, I realized, staring at the computer screen all day, under the fluorescent light was sapping all my energy.

Sleep problems & Cancer: We are meant to be exposed to sunlight during the day and dark at night. Any light at night will disrupt the sleep-wake cycle, also called the circadian rhythm. Blue light inhibits the melatonin production five times more than the red light. Low melatonin level at night will disrupt sleep. Have you noticed, how you struggle to sleep after watching a late-night movie, playing video games, or working on your smart screens? The blue lights reaching our retina confuses our body into thinking that the time is the day, a time for wakefulness. The hormone melatonin signaling night time and sleep time is suppressed. Melatonin is a powerful antioxidant and protects against cancer and infection. Working under artificial lights at night raises the risk of infection and cancer. Multiple studies have found that nurses working at night under artificial lights have an increased risk of breast cancer than those working during the day.

Macular degeneration: Our eyes have evolved to primarily deal with the sunlight which is mostly red, orange and yellow. Blue light has a short wavelength, but high frequency and energy. They readily penetrate the cornea, the lens, and reach the retina. Excess exposure to blue light can damage the light-sensitive cells in the retina. Blue light has been linked to macular degeneration- which is a common cause of age-related visual loss and blindness. The damage is gradual, and symptoms develop over the years. All the young people who are spending excess time on their smartphones, and video games – are at high risk for blindness from macular degeneration later on.

Hormonal Imbalance & metabolic problems: Blue light suppress melatonin production and stimulates cortisol production. Under natural light, the body secretes the cortisol during the day and melatonin during the night. Artificial light at night alters these cycles, and cortisol levels do not drop at night and stay elevated. These stress hormones increase blood pressure, blood sugar, and blood cholesterol. Blue light can increase hunger, carbohydrate craving, and obesity. Thus, in long-term, there is more risk of diabetes, heart disease, and stroke.

Mental problems: Long exposure to artificial lights are bad for psychological wellbeing. Blue light is addictive. I am seeing a lot of young people who have become addicted to their screens, social medical and video games. They have failed school and lost jobs. Time spend on screen leads to poor academic performance and may have contributed to the meteoric rise of Attention deficit disorders we see nationwide. Also, people get sadder and anxious when they are indoors under artificial lights. Sunlight causes the production of serotonin which helps in mood regulation. Also. People are more relaxed outdoors in natural settings. No wonder, beaches, and mountains remain the most popular vacation spots. Fluorescent lights are not continuous lights, but they are vibrating at frequencies. Many people get headaches and migraines working in them.

The harmful effects of junk light are cumulative and dose-dependent. There is no escape from the blue light as we rely on devices with screens emitting blue light. However, we can take steps to neutralize some of the risks. The best thing for health is to increase exposure to good light and reduce exposure to bad light.

How to Increase Healthy Light?

The healthy light sources are sunlight, natural fire, oil lamps, incandescent lights. It is relatively easy to increase exposure to natural light: Always try to work in a room with a window. If you have a window, open all the curtains. Move your desk close to the window and try to work in natural light. Every 30 minutes to 1 hour, walk outside. If your room has no windows, make it a priority to take scheduled minutes breaks every hour.

Go and stand outdoors for a few minutes every hour. Outdoor time will get your body adjusted to the sunlight and restore the circadian rhythm. Never look directly at the sun as it will damage the eyes. Whenever possible, work outdoors as long as weather permits. Most people do their exercises indoors, as most gyms are indoors under artificial lights. Exercise time is an excellent opportunity time to get healthy light.

Choose activities like walking, jogging, running, cycling, swimming that you can do outdoors. Pick up running, cycling, jogging outdoors. Natural light through the window is good, but not a substitute for direct sun exposure on the skin. Most glasses block the ultraviolet rays. UV-B rays are essential for the body to make vitamin D. Thus, even if you are by the window all day, there is no substitute for direct sun exposure to the skin. However, limit sun to no more than 1-2 hours as excess sun exposure increase risk of skin cancer in people with light skin. Many of us have no control over the busy weekdays. However, when you are off work on weekends, spend more time outdoors. Stockpile on outdoor exposure time when possible to offset some of the dangers of blue light exposure during the work week.

How to Reduce Junk Light?

The unhealthy light sources are a fluorescent light, LED light, and all screen lights from TV, Laptop, and Smartphone. These are all rich in blue lights. They are everywhere. If you work with a screen, add an antiglare protective layer on top of it. Reduce the brightness and contrast of your screen to the lowest setting that you can read comfortably. Adjust the color setting to more towards the red spectrum.

Download the software f.lux which allows the computer to go a night mode. I keep the night mode setting for all day. Buy good quality blue light blocking glasses. It will reduce eye strain and protect your eyes. I try to wear the blue light blocking glasses any time I am indoors working with artificial lights like the LED, and Fluorescents looking at a screen. At home, replace all the fluorescence and LED bulbs with incandescent light. At work, I shut off the room light, and use my lamp with incandescent light. You can also put a red cover over the light source so that they can block the blue rays.

Artificial light at night is a serious health hazard. The world health organization has classified night light as a carcinogen after studies showed an increased risk of cancer among night workers. Even a small amount of light at night disrupts the circadian rhythm. For a restful, restorative sleep, keep the bedroom completely dark. Shut off all artificial sources of light at night. My bedroom is pitch dark at night with special light blocking curtains. When I am traveling, I unplug all the cords of television, alarm, phone to stop all light sources at night.

A word of caution. The sun rays contain blue light which is maximum during the noon time. Blue light from the sun plays a biological role and have some beneficial effects. A short period of blue light exposure has shown to increase energy, focus, mood, and alertness. Full spectrum lights rich in blue waves are used in treating the depression associated with the Seasonal affective disorder in winter. However, the beneficial effects of blue light seem to be from short-term exposure. Think of the blue light as caffeine. A little exposure during the day is OK and even beneficial. But prolonged exposure will make you more tired, fatigue, and depressed.

In summary, humans have evolved to operate in natural sunlight. The artificial light sources especially that from the screen, LED, and fluorescents are harmful to our health. During the day, try to work near a window using natural daylight. At night, limit exposure to blue light by using blue light blocking glasses and using incandescent bulbs. Remember, it's not only plants, but humans can also get nourishment from light. Like junk food, also avoid junk light to improve your health and happiness.

Chapter 23

BEST ENVIRONMENT FOR SLEEP

Human being originated from primates in the African savannah over million years. During this vast period, human existed as a band of hunters and gatherers sleeping together on treetops or caves to avoid predators at night. The sleep environment tended to be dark, cold, and quiet. We still carry that legacy. At night, in preparation for sleep, our heart rate slows down, blood pressure drops, and the temperature cools down. For the perfect sleep, environment tries to create your own sleep cave. Here are the things you can do to ensure the best sleep environment-

Light:

The bedroom should be as dark as you can make it. Get black or dark blue or brown curtains to cover the windows. Cover all light sources in the room. Extend your arm and try to count the fingers. If you can see your fingers, the place is not dark enough. If you have a roommate or baby, and complete darkness is not possible, use an eye mask to block the lights.

Sound:

The room should be as quiet as possible. Sometimes it is not possible If you share living space or live in front of a busy street. In that case, use a table fan, or you can buy a white noise machine. Sleep is disturbed by the sudden change in noise level. Constant buzzing sound like that of white noise has less impact on sleep. Some people like me even sleep better with the sound of the fan.

Surface:

The bed surface should not be too soft, nor too hard. When I first came to the US, I was happy with how soft and luxurious the mattress was on the bed. But shortly, I developed back and neck pain. I switched to farm surface, and the pain disappeared. Most commercially available mattresses are too soft. I get my mattress from Ikea which is neither too soft nor too hard and is affordable for most. Clean bed sheets and pillow covers create a fresh feeling enabling better sleep.

Smell:

Certain smell and scent are soothing and relaxing. Lavender has been shown to decrease heart rate and blood pressure. One study showed that people sniffing lavender before bed slept longer and deeper. Other essential oils and aromas may help with sleep. The effect may vary between people. Try different products and see what works best for you.

Temperature:

Finding the right temperature for sleep is not straightforward. Most studies on sleep indicate that a temperature between 60 and 67 degrees Fahrenheit is optimal for sleeping, with temperatures above 75 degrees and below 54 degrees disruptive to sleep. But this misses a critical point. Human has slept successfully in the hot desert and cold mountains. At night, the earth becomes cooler which is also a signal for the body to prepare for sleep. This rhythm is disrupted when we stay in the temperature-controlled environment all day.

The ideal room temperature for sleep varies. Tom Rath in his book Eat, Sleep and Move explains it succinctly -" *All sleep temperatures are relative to what your body is accustomed to during the day. In summer, for example, I sleep with a warmer bedroom temperature (73 degrees) than I do during the winter (68 degrees) to conserve energy. What matters is that the temperature is two to four degrees cooler than what you are accustomed to during the day, whether it is summer or winter.* "

In addition to the colder room temperature, the core body temperature also needs to lower during sleep. For most people, it occurs naturally by the body's circadian rhythm which keeps the body at its warmest during the day and starts to lower body temperature in the evening to help us doze off.

But for people who have insomnia, their mind stays active, and the body remains warm. In a fascinating study by psychiatrist Dr. Daniel Buysse- 12 insomniacs were given a cap to wear that contained circulating water at cold temperatures. These lowered their body temperature and helped them fall and stay asleep like people without insomnia.

Many nights I have been busy doing active mental work till late in the evening. I have used cold showers to lower my body temperature rapidly and signal the body to sleep.

Sometimes too much cold can also disrupt sleep. This happens for people who get cold feet at night. If you have a cold foot, consider using socks or blankets on your feet.

Journaling and Diary Keeping:

Many times, we cannot fall asleep due to recurrent thoughts in our mind. Many times, it is best to write them down. Writing is a powerful tool. It lets us transfer our thoughts and feelings to a paper. This process transfers our angst and worries from our emotional brain (we have no control) to our rational brain which we can control. Sometimes interpersonal conflicts keep us awake. Writing a letter to resolve a dispute with another person, or to express your feelings, can be an essential tool for coping.

Try to form a habit of writing in our journal once every day, preferably before you go to bed. Keep it in a private place and make sure no one else reads it. Otherwise, you might become fearful of expressing your emotions honestly. Once, you develop this habit; you will enjoy it.

Also, many people who have obsessive streaks are always worrying about forgetting things to do the next day. For them, keeping a checklist helps. Every night, review and edit to your checklist. This will ensure that you have all the things written down and ease the pressure from memory. Journaling over time become a part of your sleep ritual. Once you write down and empty your mind, you can go to sleep in peace.

Electronic Device:

Do not keep your phone or laptop in your bedroom. If you do, then shut them off before going to sleep. Do not use your phone as an alarm. If you do, then put it on the airplane mode. The electromagnetic radiation from devices disrupts the action of hormone melatonin which the body secretes at night for sleep. Also, make sure the Wi-Fi modem is far away from the bedroom. If you can, it is best to turn off the Wi-Fi modem before sleep. This will also decrease overall radiation exposure for the entire family.

Sleep Trackers & Monitors:

Many companies have come up with a tracking device which can monitor your sleep. There are alarm clocks which constantly measure your sleep waves and only wake you up when it is least disruptive. They may be useful in the short term as you may want to know your baseline and identify your problem areas.

However, I do not recommend them for long-term use. All devices use electromagnetic radiation to track sleep. Many like the Apple watch, Fitbit require constant skin contact and emit green light. From other studies, we know that exposure to light and radiation is disruptive for sleep. Using the same logic, I advise patients to use sleep tracker only during the initial phase of diagnosis and treatment of sleep problem. Once the solution is identified, the goal should be to sleep as naturally as possible.

In summary, the sleep environment plays a crucial role in your sleep. Create your own sleep zone. Think of bats who stay in the dark, cool caves sleeping more than 16 hours each day. Make your bedroom at bedtime cooler than a day. Use air-conditioning to adjust the temperature if the room is not cold enough. Buy thick multilayered dark curtains, white noise or fan, and make your room light and sound free. Do not bring any work to the bedroom and keep it a stress-free and distraction-free zone. Remove and unplug all other electronic devices to make your room radiation free. You will be amazed at how rapidly you fall asleep, and how deep your sleep will become.

Chapter 24

TEN RULES OF GOOD SLEEP

Many of us struggle with sleep. The problems can be many. Some struggle to fall asleep at night, some to maintain sleep throughout the night, and some from too early waking. Whatever the nature of the problem, sleep deprivation weakens the mind and body and makes us vulnerable to various mental and physical diseases. Here are the ten rules of good sleep. It will be a quick synopsis of the sleep strategies that we have learned so far.

1. **Schedule Sleep**: Maintain a consistent bedtime routine. Go to bed at the same time every night. Try to keep the same sleep time even on the weekends. Following a routine will keep your body's natural sleep rhythm synchronized.

2. **Exercise daily**: Try to get some exercise during the day; as little as 20 minutes can help. Aerobics, lifting weights, power yoga, walking- any form of physical exertion will help. However, avoid heavy exercise 2 hours before sleep as the increased arousal from physical activity might make sleep difficult.

3. **Avoid alcohol, nicotine, and caffeine** before bedtime. Alcohol helps to sleep in short-term but robs the brain of deep restorative sleep in the long term. Caffeine is present in tea, coffee, and soda. Nicotine is present in cigarettes. Both caffeine and nicotine are brain stimulants, which makes one more

alert and awake while making it difficult to fall asleep.

4. **Relax before Sleep**: Do something relaxing before bedtime like taking a warm bath, reading, or listening to music. Mindfulness exercises can also help.

5. **Light Exposure during the day**. Try to get exposure to sunlight or any full spectrum bright light in the morning. Exposure to light during the day and darkness before bed will entrain your circadian rhythm to the daily light-dark cycle. This will help you stay alert and active during the day while being tired and sleepy at night.

6. **Don't eat before going to bed**. Have your dinner at least two hours before sleep time. Avoid food just before bedtime, and never have your food in the bed. A heavy meal before bedtime is difficult to digest and will also impair sleep. Also, avoid too spicy or sugary food before bed. Food rich in tryptophan like nuts, cheese, oats, beans, lentils, eggs, fish, chicken, turkey can boost sleep.

7. **Don't check emails or work on your laptop just before bed.** The mind needs to relax, and any activation will impair sleep. Avoid TV, Computer, or bright light before sleep as they inhibit the sleep-inducing hormone –melatonin.

8. **Keep your bedroom quiet, cold, and dark at night**. Adjust your thermostat to a lower temperature between 60 to 67 degrees. Use thick curtains to block light and white-noise to block sound. Remember the bedroom temperature should be lower than what

your body experience at day.

9. The bed should be used **only for sleep, and sex**. Avoiding all other activities at bed will help the body associate the bed with sleep. If you want, you can do some light reading using a bed lamp occasionally.

10. **Write your worries** before sleep. Many people bring their fears and concerns to bed and cannot stop thinking about them. Keep a journal at the bedside to write down troubling thoughts before going to bed. Transferring your ideas to a paper will prevent the repeated cycle of worrying and enable sleep.

Sleep is vital to life. Seek professional help if you struggle with sleep chronically and experience daytime fatigue. Many of the sleep problems can be resolved with the help of medications and therapy like Cognitive behavioral therapy for Insomnia. In the end, don't neglect any sleep problems, and make every effort to get good sleep for your health and wellbeing.

PART V
SLEEP APNEA

Chapter 25

WHAT IS SLEEP APNEA?

Many times, sleep problems persist in spite of following all sleep strategies and maintaining good sleep hygiene. One typical scenario is a condition called Sleep Apnea seen commonly among overweight people who snore at night. This is a severe condition which can lead to many other physical and mental disorders. Sleep Apnea requires specialized treatment, many times involving a sleep specialist and a sleep clinic.

During sleep, we lose voluntary control of our muscles. The involuntary body actions like the circulation (pumping of the heart), and digestion continues. Breathing is both voluntary and involuntary. Many times, the breath becomes shallow or pause during sleep waking the person for a brief moment momentarily disrupting regular sleep. This condition is called Sleep Apnea.

Sleep apnea can be of two types. When the apnea or pause in breathing is due to an obstruction in the airway, it is called Obstructive Sleep Apnea. When the apnea is due to a faulty signal from the brain, it is called Central sleep apnea. Central sleep apnea is a rare, but severe neurological condition and requires specialized treatment. Here we will discuss mainly obstructive sleep apnea which can be improved by lifestyle changes.

In human, airway passage (trachea) is located forward, or in front of the food passage (esophagus). This arrangement is a remnant of our evolution from aquatic life forms when organisms had a single passage for both functions. Both this passage begins in the throat which performs the complicated role of breathing, speaking, drinking and eating.

The passage for the airway is kept closed while swallowing food and drinking water to prevent aspiration. The airway passage needs to remain open in all other times including sleep to allow breathing.

During the REM sleep or the dream sleep, our muscles remain paralyzed so that we don't act on our dreams. It also has an unwanted consequence. The muscle tone of the throat and neck is lost allowing the tongue and throat muscles to relax. These are the muscles which keep the breathing passage open. For the majority, the relaxation does not pose any breathing problem. But for people with narrow breathing passage, to begin with, it adds up. When a significant amount of airway becomes narrow, it results in apnea. Apnea means cessation of breath.

The most common type of apnea is called Obstructive Sleep Apnea (OSA). Initially, the condition was called "Pickwickian syndrome" from a novel by Charles Dickens' called the "Pickwick Papers." It was based on the character Joe "…the fat boy who consumes great quantities of food and constantly falls asleep in any situation at any time of day," as Dickens wrote.

Any factor which causes narrowing of the throat like the common cold, allergies, acid reflux, weight gain, inflammation of tonsils, adenoids will narrow the breathing passage and increase the risk for OSA. Snoring is a good indicator of

OSA. The sound of snoring is produced when the air is forced to pass through a narrow-compromised breathing passage, the louder the snoring, the severe the degree of narrowing. Imagine, how a sound is produced in a whistle, or through the flute.

Dr. William C. Dement had given the best description of OSA in his book "The Promise of Sleep": "In a stunning evolutionary failure, nature endowed us with throats that tend to collapse during sleep and stop airflow but did not endow our sleeping brains to start breathing calmly. At this breathless moment, the immediate future holds only two possibilities: death or waking up to breathe. In the worst cases, no air enters the lungs for 40,50, 60 seconds, or longer. The muscles of the diaphragm struggle harder and harder against the blocked throat, without success. Carbon dioxide builds up in the bloodstream, and the level of life-giving oxygen falls precipitously. After a minute or more of the brain is panicking, suffocating, screaming out for oxygen. The skin and lips turn blue".

He continues "Just when death seems imminent, the sleeper suddenly struggles awake, and the tongue and throat muscles tighten, allowing oxygen to flood into the lungs, in a series of gasping, snorting breaths. Oxygen is restored to the blood; the fatal course is reversed. Instead of being alarmed and staying awake, the victim is immediately asleep again. After a few seconds snoring begins — and the cycle starts again, repeating hundreds and hundreds of times at night…apnea victims have no memory of their all-night life and death struggle for breath".

In OSA, the impediment of the airflow can vary in severity

from a light snoring to a loud snoring to a complete collapse. When the airway collapse is severe, blood oxygen level drops and blood carbon dioxide levels rise. It triggers neurological arousals. These arousals will not cause complete awakening and thus are rarely remembered the next day. But the repetitive waking causes sleep disruption and impairs the deep restorative sleep.

Other symptoms associated with OSA are heartburn, headaches, dry mouth, and sexual problems like impotence, and reduced libido. OSA leads to chronic oxygen deficit in the brain leading to changes in the frontal cortex and hippocampus. This oxygen deficit can cause problems in memory, concentration, problem-solving, and organizational skills.

Patients will sleep apnea also develop hypertension. However, their blood pressure does not get better with antihypertensive medications. Many also become depressed, seek psychiatric care, but do not get better with antidepressants. Unless the core issue of OSA is treated, they continue to suffer. Although OSA commonly occurs in obese middle-aged, and older adults- I have also seen young, thin people with a narrow jaw having this condition.

Chapter 26

SLEEP APNEA DIAGNOSIS AND TREATMENT

Let us study a common presentation of obstructive sleep apnea in the following case.

Paige's Problem: Paige is a 37-year-old female, mother of two young children. She has been complaining of depressed mood and fatigue. She feels tired and sleepy all day in-spite of getting 8 hours of sleep at night. She also gets angry and irritable very easily. She was overweight, gained considerable weight during pregnancy. She had been unable to lose weight following her last pregnancy and continued to be obese.

She has been snoring at night for some time. Recently it has become worse. She wakes up many times and has interrupted sleep. Her husband complains of the loud snoring and cannot sleep in the same room with her now. She has become pale and tired and complains of poor motivation. She has been feeling drowsy during the daytime.

Once she fell asleep while driving, luckily her husband was by her side and saved the day. She is now scared of driving. She was also struggling at her job. She works as an office clerk. She is struggling at work- forgetting to update the accounts, unable to organize meetings and appointments. It became so overwhelming to the point that she has been on medical leave for the last two months. She was also recently diagnosed with increased blood pressure (hypertension) by her primary care physician. She has also been experiencing heartburn and headache in the mornings. She was initially referred to me for evaluation of Major Depressive Disorder. She has seen a psychiatrist in the past and had tried many antidepressants and sleeping pills, but her condition has continued to get worse.

I suspected her having sleep apnea and referred her for a sleep study. She came back with a diagnosis of obstructive sleep apnea.

Snoring at night is a reliable indicator of sleep apnea. If one has been snoring at night, experiencing fatigue, and excessive daytime sleepiness, there is a high chance of having obstructive sleep apnea.

OSA is diagnosed with Polysomnography which a night long sleep test called. Polysomnography generally includes monitoring of the patient's airflow, blood pressure, heart activity, blood oxygen level, brain wave pattern, eye movement, and the movement of airway muscle and limbs.

The severity of the sleep apnea is determined by counting the number of apnea episodes causing arousals from sleep across the night divided by the number of hours of sleep. This index is called the Apnea-Hypopnea Index (AHI) which is useful to determine the severity of OSA and evaluate the effectiveness of treatment.

Once a diagnosis is confirmed, various treatment modalities are available for OSA. Patients are encouraged to abstain from alcohol, smoking, sedatives and muscle relaxants. Weight loss and physical training also help. These lifestyle changes are the first line of treatment. If they fail, or patients continue to have OSA in-spite of losing weight, then other options should be considered.

There are two ways to increase the airway and facilitate breathing. One is to increase the pressure of inhaled air using a Continuous Positive Airway Pressure (CPAP) machine. This will force air through the narrow-closed passages. The machine pumps-controlled stream of air through a mask is worn over the nose and or mouth. This additional pressure holds the relaxed muscles and keeps the airways open. Another approach for keeping the airway open is to use dental implants and move the lower jaw forward.

Many patients do not like to use the CPAP for life, or their OSA is too severe to get better with CPAP. They will need surgery to remove some excess tissues of the throat and increase the space for the airways. Commonly used surgical methods are the removal of the nasal turbine, tonsils, adenoids, and straightening of the nasal septum. In most severe cases all these are removed along with remodeling of the uvula, soft palate, and pharynx. Surgical methods sometimes fail when tissues grow back, and OSA ensures. In the morbidly obese, bariatric weight loss surgery can be considered.

Sleep prescription for Paige: As I suspected, her sleep study confirmed Obstructive Sleep Apnea. I educated her about the conservative approaches like avoiding alcohol, tobacco, muscle relaxants and sedatives. She was encouraged to lose weight through diet, exercise and lifestyle changes. She was also assessed by a sleep medicine specialist and was started on Continuous Positive Airway Pressure. I saw her again six months later. She looked slim, refreshed and energetic. Most of her symptoms are gone, and she felt happier than before.

Chapter 27

SLEEP APNEA PREVENTION FOR CHILDREN

As discussed in the previous chapter, Obstructive Sleep Apnea (OSA)is a serious condition which leads to multiple physical and mental problems. But the good news is that many risk factors of OSA can is preventable with lifestyle changes. The best preventive strategies begin at birth and childhood. However, it is never too late to make positive health changes. Let us review them.

Breastfeeding:

Prevention of sleep apnea begins with birth. First, every attempt should be made to breastfeed the baby. Breastfeeding offers a multitude of benefits including higher IQ levels, lower incidences of allergies, infection and can reduce baby's risk of developing diabetes, hypertension, obesity, and cancer later in life. Additionally, the sucking action involved in breastfeeding is essential for the formation of tongue and throat muscles. Dr. Brian Palmer, a dentist, asserts that bottle feeding may be responsible for the increased cases of snoring and sleep apnea in children and adults. Palmer writes *"Anything placed in a child's mouth excessively other than the mother's breast can impact tooth alignment. While the soft breast adapts to the shape of the infant's mouth, anything firm requires the mouth to do the adapting. Besides, during breastfeeding, the tongue moves in a peristaltic motion underneath the breast. This motion is critical for the proper development of swallowing, alignment of the teeth, and the shaping of the hard palate.".*

Palmer also explains, "*Another key point about breastfeeding is that all the perioral musculature gets involved. Breastfeeding is a complex process needing coordinated efforts by all the muscles of the mouth and jaw. Infants have to 'work' all the muscles during breastfeeding. Example: Farmers who milk cows by hand, have strong hands, arms, and shoulders. Those who use milking machines, don't!*"

Other studies have shown that bottle feeding and the use of pacifies encourage the formation of high palate, narrow arch and malocclusion of teeth. The high palate, narrow dental arches, retracted lower jaw, and thick neck is the risk factors of Sleep apnea. Another dentist Dr. Arthur Strauss asserts that poor diet over generations and the lack of breastfeeding is giving rise to the tsunami of dental and sleep problems among children. It is no wonder that more and more children are getting braces for proper teeth alignment.

Nutrient Dense Food:

Children during their growing years require nutrient-rich food. Currently, there is a phobia of cholesterol and fat. The tendency to give children a low-fat diet and processed food can impair their bone and mouth development. Fat is vital for children. That's why the milk from a healthy mother has about 50 to 60 percent of its energy (calories) as fat.

Children need this extra fat for their growing brain and body. The brain, nerves, skin, lining of internal organs, eyes, hormones – all are made from saturated fat.

Dr. Weston Price, a dentist (also hauled as the Darwin of nutrition) traveled across the world to study the reasons for dental problems. He found that studied the primitive cultures across Europe, Africa, America, New Zealand and Australia. He discovered that cultures eating their traditional diets had near perfect teeth- free of cavities, perfect teeth positioning, and a wide jaw with broad maxillary and mandibular arches. The primitive people he studied ate local food, free from any preservation, refinement, and processing.

However, as people started eating a western diet composed of refined grains, sugar, canned food, processed fats and oil, their tooth deteriorated. They had less bioavailable calcium, vitamin D, vitamin A, vitamin K2 and other nutrients in their diet. Primitive people adopting western diet in few generations developed rampant tooth decay, infectious illness, and degenerative conditions. Children born to parents who had adopted the so-called civilized diet had crowded and crooked teeth, narrowed faces, deformities of bone structure and reduced immunity to disease.

Madhusree Mukherjee, in her book 'The Land of Naked People" narrates a similar experience among the aboriginals of Andaman Islands. The aboriginals who were observed to have the perfect body and strong teeth by the early colonial accounts, developed malnourishment, poor tooth, tuberculosis and other problems since adopting the civilized diet rich in refined white rice as offered by the Indian government.

Vitamin D and Sun exposure:

Vitamin D is crucial for the absorption of calcium in the intestine. It is essential for the formation of bones and teeth. Vitamin D is difficult to get from the diet alone. The human body is designed to made vitamin D through their skin using the sunlight. Children need sun exposure, but it should be regulated based on their skin color and weather.

However, excess sun exposure in light skin people can predispose them to skin cancer. Lack of vitamin D has been attributed to poor teeth and jaw development and can predispose to narrow jaw, high arch, crowded teeth. All the above are risk factors for sleep apnea.

However regular sunlight may not be an option during the winter months, and for those living near the poles. Vitamin D supplementation is a viable option, and now pediatricians are routinely recommending vitamin D supplementation for newborns and children. Good sources of vitamin D are cod liver oil, organ meats, pastured milk, egg yolk, butter, ghee and wild fish.

Chapter 28

SLEEP APNEA PREVENTION FOR ADULTS

Adults have fully developed bone and musculature. Protective factors like for children like breastfeeding, nutrient-dense food, and vitamin D are not applicable to adults as their jaw is already formed and fixed. However, not all is lost. The biggest problem for a most adult is a sedentary lifestyle and overweight. People with a narrow jaw and those overweight are at high risk. Following are the lifestyle changes that will protect as well as reduce the sufferings from sleep apnea.

Exercise and Physical training:

Exercise promotes the deeper and most rejuvenating stages of sleep. Exercise also reduces daytime sleepiness. Exercise also reduces the night time apneic spells that OSA patients experience. This improvement was noticed irrespective of the person's baseline weight. BMI. Thus, both obese and non-obese patients can improve their sleep and reduce OSA symptoms through exercise.

Exercise also improves muscle tone. Remember, we always need a muscle tone to keep the airway lumen open. Any factor decreasing the muscle tone, will cause laxity and predispose to lumen collapse and OSA. Reduced muscle tone in old people, pregnant and postpartum women make them at risk for developing OSA.

Weight Loss:

Weight loss is a significant risk factor for sleep apnea. Losing weight decreases blood pressure, blood sugar, blood cholesterol. Weight loss also reduces the risks of heart attack, stroke, diabetes and other ailments. Losing excess weight is the first step in both the prevention and treatment of sleep apnea. As we gain weight, there is fat accumulation both inside and outside our body. Fat accumulation in throat narrows the airway. When people lose weight, their snoring and sleep apnea improves dramatically. A ten to twenty percent weight reduction can eliminate many of the symptoms of sleep apnea.

Avoid muscle relaxants:

Any medication that can relax muscles should be avoided. These are brain depressants like sleeping pills, alcohol, antipsychotics, and painkillers. Consult with your doctor and determine if any of your prescribed medication is contributing to the snoring and OSA.

Avoid Cigarette smoking:

Chronic cigarette smoking causes narrowing of the airways which makes OSA worse. Cigarette smoking is a chemical irritant and causes inflammation of the airways which can lead to fluid retention. The inflammation and fluid retention decrease the airway and increases the risk for snoring and subsequent OSA.

Sleeping on the sides:

According to sleep expert Dr. Steven Park, "Modern humans on a refined diet have smaller jaw than it was hundreds of years ago. A narrow jaw leads to crowding of the airway. The tongue, which grows to its' normal size, takes up relatively too much space, and when lying on your back, falls back almost completely. Dr. Steven Park, a sleep expert, recommends sleeping on the sides for OSA patients. The only thing that's keeping you from obstructing is some muscle tension when you inhale. The problem happens when you go into deeper stages of sleep, where by definition, your muscles must relax. In REM sleep (the dreaming stage), all your muscles are relaxed completely, except for your eyes and diaphragm. " During the dreaming phase, sleep apnea patients stop breathing, then they take a few breaths in against a closed throat, wake up and roll over."

Most people instinctively choose the posture that's best for their breathing. Most people with sleep apnea choose to sleep on their stomach or sides. Sleeping on the sides is better than stomach as this allows for full expansion of chest and abdomen during breathing.

PART VI
SLEEP FOR BABIES

Chapter 29

WHY BABIES CRY ?

Sleep requirement for babies is different from that of the adults. The circadian clock which tells adults when to sleep and wake is not developed in babies. That is why babies sleep and wake both during day and night. And, because babies cannot verbalize their needs, they cry a lot which is their way of communicating distress. Understanding the cries of the baby will help parents meet the needs of a baby. As a child psychiatrist, I firmly believe in providing a secure attachment and nurturing to the babies while growing up. This is protective against future anxiety, depression and stress disorders.

Many parents struggle with the sleep of their baby. They spend hours trying to make the baby sleep, and then anxiously monitor her. Many times, babies will wake up in the middle of the night and start crying. Parents often struggle to figure out the cause of crying and how to soothe her. Crying of a baby can become dangerous as many cases of child abuse happened when one of the parents lost control after hours of failed attempt to soothe a crying baby at night. To figure out the sleep needs of a baby, we need to understand why babies cry and what they want.

As a new father, my sleep is often disturbed by the cry of my son. It seems babies cry too long and far too often, and often it does not make sense. Humans are purposeful mammals. Everything we do serve a purpose- be it work, obligation, leisure, fun, survival. Does the cry of a baby have a meaning, or it is just an anomaly? The healthy newborn announces her arrival to the world with a loud cry. Babies have no language. They can only express themselves with sounds and gestures. Cries of the baby serve many purposes. Mammalian babies are born helpless and week. They make an excellent target for the predators as they have no defense. The cry is often a call for help to summon the caregivers against any real or imaginary danger. As I write this, my toddler plays on the floor near my feet. I get up and say to him that I am leaving now and walk out and close the door. Suddenly, the squeal of joy stops. The toys are dropped. He stands and runs to the door and cries. I stand on the other side of the door, wait a moment, and then open the door. He lunges to my feet. I pick him up on my lap and soothe him. He stops crying.

Cries of the baby if sustained should never be ignored. Contrary to popular myth, prolonged crying is never helpful. The old belief that the cries make the heart and lung stronger is wrong. The only time cries are good is at birth. The loud cries help to clear up the fluid from the lungs of the baby and ease its transition to a terrestrial environment from the aquatic milieu of the mother's womb. Tears of joy and tears of sorrow for the adults are different physiological mechanisms not to be confused with the heart wrenching shrill cries of the babies. There are many reasons which will make a baby cry. Babies have immature temperature control. They are more prone to get heat and cold. Babies will cry if it is too hot or too cold for them. Reports of babies dying by heat after being locked in the car are not uncommon. Babies can die of cold if not adequately clothed and heated.

Also, no one likes to be wet. Same is with babies. They will cry if the diaper becomes too wet, or if they soil their clothes.

Babies also need physical touch. They need to be embraced, held, cuddled, and touched. Constant physical contact with a caregiver, also called kangaroo care has shown to improve survival in early born babies in the hospital. In Harry Harlow's controversial experiment- baby monkeys preferred the mother figure which provided a physical touch more than the mother figure which provided food. Babies also cry when they are hungry. Give them a bottle of milk or mother's breast, and it will sooth them. They also cry when they are thirsty. As most houses use Air-conditioning and heater for temperature control, babies can become dehydrated. Feed ample of fluids to keep the baby hydrated. Many parents use a pacifier to soothe babies. Some use is ok, but too much use of pacifier interferes with the proper alignment of teeth and formation of the dental arches.

Babies need a lot of sleep. Half of their sleep contains dreams. The dream sleep, also known as REM sleep is the longest at birth and decreases as we age. Babies sometimes will wake up from sleep and cry. Scary dreams bother them more and they will cry during or after sleep as an expression of fear. They need to be close to the caregiver to the soothed and reassured for their safety. That is why it is risky to make a newborn sleep in a different room in the first year of their life. The American Pediatric Association has recently changed its recommendations and now advices that parents sleep their newborn in the same room but on a separate bed or bassinet close to the parents' bed.

Some parents believe that crying to sleep is OK. Nothing can be further from the truth. Yes, it is true that babies left on their own will eventually stop crying and sleep. Babies will learn this routine and sleep finally. But they will also learn another lesson. "When I cry, no one comes for help." These babies growing up will struggle to ask for help.

The American culture emphasizes individualism and parents are encouraged to make their children independent as early as possible. This is good in theory only when done in the right order. Independence can only be learned after one knows how to be dependent. Humans are social animals. No one can survive too long in isolation. True independence can only come after someone has learned how to trust and depend on others. An unheeded crying baby will be forced to learn to be independent early on. But she will also learn that when she asks for help, no one will come. As an adult, she will struggle to ask for help and trust others. Trust problem will breed insecurity in her relationships. People with insecure attachment are at risk for depression, anxiety, paranoia, and other mental health problems.

Stages of Psychosocial development by Erik Erikson:

Age	Psychological Crisis	Significant Relationship	Existential Question
0-2 years	Trust vs. Mistrust	Mother	Can I trust the world?
2-4 years	Autonomy vs. Doubt	Parents	Is it Ok to be me?
4-5 years	Initiative vs. Guilt	Family	Is it Ok to do, move & Act?

In summary, we feel sad, miserable, pained, stressed, frustrated, depressed, angry, when we hear a baby cry. It disturbs our peace of mind and equilibrium. This is because that is the exact purpose. Babies are born defenseless and helpless and rely on the caregivers for their survival. If unheeded, the cry will go up, to summon help at any cost.

The typical reason for cries can range from hunger, thirst, and cold, hot, impending danger, scary dreams, loneliness, and for physical touch. If the cries of the baby do not stop after taking care of all the above, there may be medical problems. Common ones can be fever, cold, allergy, constipation, and abdominal colic. Some babies also experience tooth and bone pains. There may be serious ailments- like infection, trauma, abuse, injury, and others which will make babies cry inconsolably. If this happens, consult your doctor or take the baby to the nearest emergency room or urgent care. Take any cry lasting more than few minutes seriously and heed to it.

Chapter 30

WHERE SHOULD BABIES SLEEP?

Many immigrants living in the US are baffled when told that their babies should sleep alone. This goes against most traditional and cultural norms. Human babies have been sleeping with their parents from time immemorial like other people in Asian and more traditional cultures. Making the baby sleep alone is a western construct, and that too a recent one. Even as early as 200 years ago, the babies in the western countries used to sleep with their caregivers in the same room.

The media and many health professionals routinely scare the parents by saying that making the infant sleep with them will increase the risk of Sudden Infant Death Syndrome (SIDS). But the truth is more nuanced. The sudden infant death syndrome is the number one killer of infants in US. No one knows for sure, what causes it.

SIDS, also called cot death or crib death is the sudden unexplained death of an infant. The cause of death remains unknown after all investigations. SIDS usually occurs during sleep. Infants die in sleep, without any warning. Some studies have found that infants sleeping with their parents have a higher risk of SIDS than those sleeping alone. These findings are frequently quoted by hospitals and pediatricians to discourage parents from sleeping alongside their babies. But in those studies, the cases where infants died, there were also other factors involved like parental alcoholism, drug abuse, obesity, etc.

Global research findings show that the rate of SIDS is lowest in countries where babies sleep with their parents. The United States where babies sleep alone has the highest rate of SIDS-2 per 1000 live births. SIDS is lowest in Asia; the SIDS rate in Japan is 0.3 per 1000 births, 0.03 per 1000 births in Hong Kong, and even lower in China.

However, bed sharing can be dangerous to the infant under certain circumstances. If one of the parent is obese, alcoholic, abusing drugs- then there is a chance they can roll over their baby, and may be too inebriated to hear the baby's cries and may suffocate them. Also, what complicates the matter is the type of mattress commonly used in an American household. Most mattresses are too soft and are of poor quality. They contribute to back pain and poor sleeping postures.

In contrast, the Asian countries use a relatively firmer surface for sleep. Traditional Japanese use tatami mats or much thinner cotton futons which they lay on the floor to sleep. In India, I remember my parents getting the weaver, who will weave a small futon for our bed using cotton. Around half of the children in America are now not raised by their two biological parents. This is a matter of concern at night during sleep. The step-parent who is not biologically related may have a lower threshold of tolerance for the baby which may put the infant at risk.

Co-sleeping and bed sharing with the infant also promote exclusive breastfeeding which is protective against SIDS. Breastfeeding is best for the infants. It has numerous health benefits and is superior to any formula or food. World health organization recommends exclusive breastfeeding for the first 4-6 months and to continue breastfeeding till around two years. Making a baby sleep in a different room disrupts the breastfeeding and leads to early weaning.

The ideal way to breastfeed is to feed on demand and not on a schedule. That is how babies have been brought up in the traditional societies and among other primates. The biology of infants has not changed since the time human evolved from primates around 6 million years ago. All primate babies cling to their mothers. Human babies have been sleeping with their mothers for care, comfort, milk in close physical contact for the entire length of human history. Even today, the majority of babies around the world sleep alongside with their mothers.

The Western society values independence, initiative, and risk-taking; all the traits which will make one successful in a capitalistic and democratic society. These values are reflected in the child-rearing practices where parents try to make their children as independent as possible, and as early as possible. The cultural notion is- earlier the babies learn to live alone and by themselves, more independent they will become. However, studies on human infant attachment have revealed contrary results. It shows that the babies who get adequate love, care, and nurturing from their parents develop a secure and healthy attachment to their parents.

Secure attachment leads to well-balanced adults who have less emotional problems later on. One key component of secure attachment is for the baby to feel safe when growing up. If a baby cries, it is essential for parents to pick up and soothe the baby quickly. If the baby is in a different room, and parents don't hear the cry- the baby may be crying for a while until it gets any relief. Even worse, the baby may cry to sleep getting the message that in distress there is no help.

When it comes to child care, one has to be careful about the recommendations. Many childrearing practices promoted in the western society and endorsed by the medical association have been proven harmful. For example, until a few decades ago formula milk was touted as a healthier choice than breast milk by the manufacturers, and the doctors used to endorse it. Then there was another advice to let a baby cry. Mothers were encouraged not to tend to their babies immediately and not to soothe them. This harmful practice still followed by many causes emotional distress to the babies and impedes attachment to caregivers.

Then there was the practice of keeping the mother and the baby separate after birth. Hospital routinely placed the babies in a different room. Now we know that the first hour after birth is extremely crucial for the bonding between the baby the mother and they should be kept in contact during that time. The American Pediatric Association used to advocate separate sleeping room for the babies. It changed its position in light of the new research and now recommends that babies sleep in the same room as parents, but on a separate surface like a bassinet. This is better as it will provide room for skin to skin contact between the baby and the mother.

Many parents put a television in the baby's room to stop them from crying and help them sleep. This is extremely harmful as the light from the TV will disrupt the sleep which is vital for a baby's growth. Another practice is the use of radio transmitters or camera in babies' room so that the parents can monitor the baby from their bedroom. This is unnecessary, expensive, and makes a simple process of sleep somewhat complicated. Just add another futon in the bedroom and let the baby sleep there in front of your watchful eyes and free from the electronic distractions.

Child rearing is a personal choice. The sleeping arrangement for babies and adults is a decision guided by the cultural norms and societal expectations. From the standpoint of the baby's health and biology- infants should stay as close to their caregivers as possible both during the day and the night. It might not be possible all the times in the urban setting where a mother has to leave for work. But it is still the best for the baby, and every effort should be made towards it.

Chapter 31

BEST SLEEP ENVIRONMENT FOR BABIES

All parents want the best for their babies. Even before the baby is born, they shop, arrange, and decorate a room for the baby. They buy a separate crib, monitor, camera, screen and other gazettes marketed to them. Although parents start with the right intentions, many of these purchases are unnecessary, and some outright harmful. Here are the fundamental concepts for babies' sleep as per child sleep expert Joseph McKenna-

1. Safety for babies begins even before their birth. No smoking by mother, or by others near the mother. The toxic fumes inhaled by a mother reaches the fetus through blood. Exposure to toxic fumes harms the embryo inside the womb. Same is valid for alcohol which harms the unborn fetus.

2. Breastfeeding protects infants from many health dangers like sudden infant death syndrome and other newborn diseases. Infants should sleep close to an informed, breastfeeding, committed mother.

3. Infants should always sleep on their backs, on firm surfaces, on clean surfaces, in the absence of (secondhand) smoke, under light (comfortable) blanketing, and their heads should never be covered.

4. The bed should not have any stuffed animals or pillows around the infant and never should an infant be placed to sleep on top of a pillow or otherwise soft bedding.

5. Sheepskins or other fluffy material and especially beanbag mattresses should never be used with infants. Waterbeds can be especially dangerous to infants too, and no matter the type of mattress, it should always tightly intersect the bed-frame to leave no gaps or space.

6. Infants should never sleep on couches or sofas with or without adults as they can slip down (face first) into the crevice or get wedged against the back of a couch where they may suffocate.

7. At night, infants should sleep in the same room and very close either in the same bed or an attached surface, so the constant skin to skin contact is possible. This will also ensure that the infant will be able to breastfeed on demand. It will lower the stress and anxiety level for both the mother and the baby and is protective against SIDS.

8. However, it may not be safe for the babies to share the bed with parents who are abusing alcohol and drugs, who are morbidly obese, who are taking sedative or sleeping pills at night, and who are not biologically related to the baby.

In summary, the need for babies to sleep close to the mother is essential in the first year of life when the risk for infant mortality is highest. As the baby grows and learns to vocalize and speak, they can be transferred to their room gradually. A safe and nurturing sleep environment becomes crucial for the baby's attachment and development. Parents have to be careful and committed.

PART VII
SLEEP SUPPLEMENTS

Chapter 32

WHY SUPPLEMENTS

Supplements have a long history in sleep. The role of sleep in health was recognized from the earliest times. All ancient healing systems like those of Indians, Chinese, Greeks discusses remedies for sleep problems. Unfortunately, there is a lot of confusion on sleep products, and supplements. Although there are various sleep medications on the market, it is best to use them as a last resort for their highly addictive potential, and long-term side effects.

Many safe natural supplements exist for sleep which can be as good as medications but without the side effects. Unfortunately, most doctors do not promote natural supplements. Here are two main reasons. First, natural remedies are less potent, and slow to work - and therefore unsuitable for patients in acute crisis or severe distress. Secondly, most physicians are not trained in complementary and alternative treatment, and therefore don't feel comfortable to endorse them.

Fortunately, this is changing as new research is highlighting the safety and efficacy of natural remedies, many conventional allopathic practices are embracing them. In my previous article, I have discussed four commonly used sleep supplements namely Magnesium, Melatonin, Tryptophan/5 HTP, and GABA. For many patients, these can be too strong or less effective. Fortunately, there are numerous herbal products along with vitamins and minerals available for sleep.

Here, I will discuss the most commonly used over the counter products that can promote sleep. I will give a brief overview of supplements with common dosage, indication, and side effects. When doubt, always seek professional guidance.

Chapter 33

MAGNESIUM

Magnesium: is a vital mineral for the body and plays a role in more than 300 cellular processes in the body. Magnesium deficiency is becoming a serious health hazard as around 50 percent, or half of the American population may be getting inadequate magnesium in their diet. Magnesium is essential for all muscle function including the heart. Magnesium deficiency will cause restlessness, anxiety and sleep problems. Our modern living is to blame for this. Magnesium is an anti-stress mineral.

When we experience stress, the body loses magnesium. The more the food is processed, the magnesium is lost. Intensive agriculture practices like use of fertilizers, pesticides and other chemicals also deplete the magnesium in the soil. Thus, it becomes crucial to take magnesium as a dietary supplement to balance this loss. Luckily, magnesium is a safe mineral with no serious side effects. If you take more magnesium that your body needs, you will excrete the magnesium through stool, and experience diarrhea.

There are various forms of magnesium available in the market. Avoid magnesium oxide which is ineffective for sleep. All other forms of magnesium like magnesium glycinate, magnesium threonate, magnesium taurate, and magnesium citrate will aid sleep. Among them, the most potent magnesium salt is the Magnesium L-Threonate. It is the most bioavailable form of magnesium and has the highest absorption in the brain. However, it is expensive. The standard dose is 2000 mg 1 hour before sleep. Magnesium Taurate is another excellent form of magnesium used mostly for cardiovascular health and heart problems. It can be used at a dose between 150 and 300 mg.

Magnesium Glycinate also contains glycine in addition to magnesium which promotes sleep. You can start at 200 mg bedtime and increase to 400 mg as needed. Magnesium Citrate, another commonly used form, is available both as tablet and powder. For the tablet, you can start at 150 mg, and increase to 400 mg as needed.

I prefer the powder form, available as Natural Vitality Natural Calm Anti-Stress Magnesium Drink. Take 1 to 2 teaspoons in water before sleep.

Stay away from Magnesium Oxide which is inexpensive and works the least. It is poorly absorbed and mostly lost in the stool, resulting in diarrhea. Magnesium Oxide has medicinal use as a short-term laxative, as it relieves constipation. Also, it is an excellent antacid and can be used for acid reflux. However, it cannot be used to correct magnesium deficiency in the body and is ineffective as a sleep aid.

Chapter 34

MELATONIN

Melatonin is a hormone which is secreted by the pituitary gland when we are exposed to darkness. It is a potent antioxidant and helps in the recovery and healing of the brain. After you take melatonin, avoid the bright light from the computers, smartphones, and television. Remember, melatonin cannot work unless your eyes are exposed to darkness for at least an hour.

Historically human has been sleeping within 4 hours after sunset. This only changed hundred years ago with the advent of cheap artificial light. Our body evolved to have exposure to a few hours' darkness before sleep. This darkness stimulates the posterior pituitary to secrete melatonin. As melatonin level rises, we feel sleepier.

Bright light suppresses melatonin, and amongst the light waves, blue light causes the maximum suppression of melatonin. Many times, we have to work on the screen at night. On those occasions use blue light blocking eyeglasses and turn your screen into night mode for night work. This will get rid of most of the melatonin-suppressing blue light. Melatonin is useful for those who have irregular sleeping hours. It will help those who travel frequently and suffer from jet lags and sleep problem due to change in time zones. Melatonin decreases the time for the onset of sleep.

Melatonin can be taken from a dose of 1 mg to a maximum of 5 mg on a regular basis. Melatonin is a hormone secreted by the posterior pituitary.

Melatonin although safe, can adversely react with many hormones in the body. First, although no negative feedback loop has been identified, there remains a theoretical risk of the body getting dependent on the outside melatonin and stops secreting its melatonin.

Secondly, melatonin suppresses the sex hormones and can delay puberty in children. Also, sudden stoppage of melatonin in children can lead to precocious puberty. Other side effects are headaches, dizziness, nausea, and drowsiness.

Chapter 35

TRYPTOPHAN & 5 HTP

Serotonin Precursors like tryptophan and 5 hydroxytryptophan (5HTP) play an important role in sleep. Serotonin is an essential neurotransmitter in the brain playing a crucial role in mood, anxiety, stress, and sleep. Many of the antidepressants work by rebalancing the serotonin pathway. For example, the well-known Prozac increases serotonin levels in the brain by decreasing its absorption inside cells, thus making more serotonin available in the synapses.

Prescription drugs are more powerful in increasing the serotonin levels as they are designed to cross the blood-brain barrier. We can also increase serotonin levels in the brain by eating food rich in tryptophan (turkey, egg, cheese) which is a precursor for serotonin. The good bacteria in your gut (probiotics) convert tryptophan into 5 hydroxytryptophan (5 HTP), which in turn is converted to Serotonin, and finally serotonin is converted to melatonin. Hence, directly taking Tryptophan and 5 HTP supplements (which are the raw materials for serotonin) can raise the serotonin levels in the body.

However, 90% of the serotonin is made in the gut and is used by the nerves of the gut, and very little can cross the blood-brain barrier. These may not be enough for treating severe depression or debilitating anxiety, but maybe enough for managing sleep problems. Thus, taking either tryptophan or 5TP will help in sleep. Now, which one to choose? Both have their merits and demerits.

Tryptophan is safer, as any excess amount is used by the body to make the vitamin Niacin. But this also makes it slower to work, as only 1 percent of tryptophan is available to produce serotonin.

5 HTP supplements work quicker and are more powerful, as they are the directly converted into serotonin using Magnesium, Zinc, Vitamin C, Vitamin B6. However, both tryptophan and 5 HTP should not be taken together, nor combined with any other drug or supplement which increases serotonin levels in the body.

Also, people with a cyclical mood disorder like bipolar should never take 5 HTP or Tryptophan in isolation, as it may trigger a manic episode. On the other hand, those with a purely depressive or anxiety disorders may notice an improvement in symptoms with 5 HTP and Tryptophan. The typical dose of Tryptophan for sleep is L- tryptophan 500 mg to 1000 mg. The standard dosage for 5 HTP is 50 mg to 200 mg 1-hour before sleep.

Chapter 36

GABA

GABA stands for Gamma Amino Butyric Acid. It is an inhibitory neurotransmitter to the brain. GABA can be taken as a dietary supplement. It acts through the same GABA receptor as Xanax, Valium, and Alcohol does. GABA supplements are used for anxiety, stress, and sleep. GABA can be especially useful for people who have been using alcohol for a long time before sleep, and now wants to come off alcohol, but are unable to fall asleep.

Gabapentin, a prescription drug that increases GABA level is the brain, is also used to treat alcohol addiction. For those habituated on Xanax, and Valium- GABA can be a healthier substitute. But GABA has a dark side. GABA is a brain depressant. GABA can also inhibit the frontal lobe which is the site for learning and memory. Thus, it may be unsuitable for students, and elderly with memory problems. Additionally, GABA can cause disinhibition.

Many parents have reported that their children have become more aggressive, violent and disruptive on GABA. Hence, GABA is not for all and needs careful monitoring. GABA is readily available in the health store. Usually comes at a dose of around 700 mg. 1 tablet per day to a maximum of 2 tablets per day is the recommended dose for most brands.

GABA should be taken at an empty stomach for better absorption. Ideally, take them 2 hours after meals, and 1 hour before sleep for best results. Regular GABA supplements, however, does not readily cross the blood-brain barrier. This makes GABA supplements less potent.

Phenibut, a structural analog to GABA, crosses the blood-brain barrier. Phenibut is used as a prescription drug in Eastern Europe and Russia. It is available online in the US and is unregulated. One popular sleep aid, called KAVINACE contains Phenibut, Taurine, and Vitamin B6. However, beware that Phenibut has addictive potential, and, can be abused as a recreational drug to get high.

Chapter 37

HERBAL REMEDIES

Valerian Root: Herbal remedies have been used from the beginning of medicine. Ancient healing traditions like the Indian (Ayurveda), Chinese, Greek mentions several herbs to help with sleep. Typical among them which has stood the test of time are Valerian Root, Passionflower, Lemon balm, Chamomile.

Among herbs, Valerian is the most popular one and has been used as a sleep aid since classical times. Hippocrates mentioned it in his health treatise. Galen prescribed it for sleep 2 thousand years ago. Valerian increases the level of GABA in the brain. It can bring a sense of calm, relaxation and promote deep sleep at night.

However, valerian can cause side effects of nausea, headaches, unrest, and dizziness. Some people may react very strongly to valerian like a Xanax and valium, and develop hangover the next day, and a reduction in cognition. It is advisable not to drive or operate heavy machinery after taking valerian. The typical dose for insomnia is around 500 mg 1 hour before sleep.

Other Essential herbs:

Passionflower is another relaxing herb and is used in combination with Valerian root in many sleep aid formulations. It also helps with anxiety and relaxation.

Lemon balm is another ancient herb work that through the GABA. It has a soothing effect on the brain. It also improves memory along with sleep. Lemon balm essential oil is also used in aromatherapy.

Chamomile is consumed as a tea to help with sleep. Also, chamomile tea can also assist in reducing inflammation, in improving digestion, and in relieving a sore throat.

Ayurvedic Herbs

Herbs had been used in India for past thousand years to treat various ailments. With the rise of western interest in Yoga and meditation- there is a surge in the research and marketing of Ayurvedic herbs. The most studied herbs for mental ailments and insomnia are Ashwagandha, Brahmi, and Shankhpushpi.

Ashwagandha, also called Withania Somnifera reduces chronic stress by decreasing the blood cortisol or the stress hormone level. Ashwagandha is an energizing herb, which reduces anxiety, and relaxes the mind for sleep.

Shankhapushpi is another brain rejuvenation herb which improves blood circulation and helps with insomnia.

Brahmi, also called Bacopa, is a memory booster. Legend has that the ancient seers used Brahmi to memorize all the Vedic knowledge which was orally transmitted over the generations. Brahmi is a brain tonic and promotes healthy nerve function. It can also act as a tranquilizer and aid in sleep.

In summary herbal remedies have been used for centuries for sleep. They are generally safe and can be taken without a doctor's supervision. However, they also have week effects. They are best made in combination with other sleep aids like magnesium, GABA, and melatonin. Many over the counter sleep supplemental formulations combine them with other agents.

Chapter 38

VITAMINS FOR SLEEP

Nutritional deficiency of certain minerals and vitamins can also cause sleep problems. For example, B group of vitamins are essential for nerve function. Several B vitamins help in the regulation of sleep mainly by acting through the tryptophan-serotonin pathway. Poor diet and stress may lead to deficiencies which can be corrected by supplements. Here are the most common ones,

Inositol: It is a B-vitamin which boost the action of serotonin and has a natural calming effect on the body. It is beneficial if your sleep problems are due to anxiety and obsessive thoughts. A double-blinded study found inositol as effective as the commonly prescribed medication fluvoxamine/Luvox in reducing the panic attacks and anxiety in patients. It is available in both powder and tablet form.

Powder form is preferred as you can go up on the dose. Inositol is very safe, and the dose ranges from 1 gram to 18 grams per day. The prescription for insomnia is about 2 grams at night 2 hours before sleep. It is easily tolerated without side effects. Its effects are potentiated by taking it with choline or choline-rich food like egg yolk and animal fat. In addition to brain function, inositol also helps with acne, menstrual problems, and metabolic problems. However, inositol takes some time to work. You may need to take inositol for at least a month before noticing a benefit.

B3: Niacin (B3) is mostly known for the disease pellagra caused by its deficiency which can cause dementia, dermatitis, diarrhea, insomnia and general weakness. Niacin is needed for every cell of the body. The exact way how niacin causes insomnia is unknown. Theoretically, we know that more than ninety percent of the tryptophan in the diet is used to make niacin. Thus, an adequate level of niacin in the body will free up more tryptophan for the serotonin and melatonin production.

B6: Another B vitamin called pyridoxine (B6) is needed in the conversion of tryptophan to serotonin. Women taking oral contraceptives or hormone replacement therapy may secrete more tryptophan metabolites in their urine and become deficient in B6. Supplementation with vitamin B6 can mitigate some of these problems.

Vitamin B12, B9 (folate) and B6 deficiency can also cause restless leg syndrome leading to sleep problems. Since vitamin B is water soluble, there is less risk of side effects. It may be a good idea to take a vitamin B supplement containing all the vitamin B types along with vitamin C for general wellbeing.

Vitamin D: The sunshine vitamin is a hormone that plays a vital role in immunity, cancer prevention, depression, bone health. Low levels of vitamin D are associated with increased sickness. Vitamin D supplementation in the morning can help with sleep. Vitamin D supplementation in the morning along with melatonin at night helps in the regulation of the circadian rhythm.

Vitamin D levels are easier to check, and your primary care doctor can order it for you. Generally, levels over 60 ng/ml are recommended. Based on your level, consider taking Vitamin D3 at a dose of 1000 IU to 5000 IU in the morning. However, whenever you take vitamin D3 doses higher than 1000 IU, always add Vitamin K2 200 mcg along with it to prevent calcium deposition in the blood vessels.

Chapter 39

AMINO ACIDS, PROBIOTICS & IRON

AMINO ACIDS

There are two amino acids Glycine and Theanine which can bring rapid sleep onset. One is Glycine of animal source, and the other is Theanine derived from tea.

Glycine is an amino acid produced by the body and is an inhibitory neurotransmitter like GABA. It dilates the blood vessels, reduces the core body temperature, and prepares the body for sleep. Glycine also helps in daytime wakefulness and reduces fatigue. Chief dietary sources of glycine are high protein food like eggs and red meat. When taken as a supplement, the typical dosage is 1 to 3 grams 1 hour before sleep.

Theanine is derived as an extract tea. It is present in both black and green tea. Although tea is stimulating as it contains caffeine, L-theanine has a calming and sedative effect. Theanine also works if sleep problems are due to restless leg movements at night. The advantage of Theanine is its rapid onset of action. It works by reducing anxiety and promotes sleep within 30 minutes of intake. A typical dose of Theanine is 100 to 200 mg before bedtime

Probiotics:

The healthy bacteria in our gut produce serotonin which is helpful in sleep. Without this tryptophan (which is the raw material for serotonin) cannot be converted into serotonin. If you have chronic constipation, chronic diarrhea or irregular bowel movement, you may have too many harmful bacteria in your gut. Taking a probiotic supplement can raise the level of good bacteria. You can also get probiotics from fermented food like yogurt, kefir, kombucha, sauerkraut, and kimchi.

Iron:

Many people move their legs at night. This causes sleep problems to them as well as their partners. The medical term for it is Restless Leg Syndrome (RLS). Iron deficiency is a common cause for RLS. Its good idea to check your iron levels if you move too much in the bed at night. Low iron levels can be treated by eating iron rich food like red meat, liver, eggs, and chicken. Most vegetarian sources are deficient in iron, and the addition of iron supplements will help. Also, remember to take adequate amounts of vitamin C as found in citrus fruits like orange and lemon juice to increase the iron absorption.

Chapter 40

HOW TO CHOOSE SLEEP SUPPLEMENTS?

Now we have covered all the commonly used supplements for sleep. How to decide which supplement is right for you. Which supplement to start first and how to proceed. Experts differ, and there is no universal consensus. Here I will give you a rough layout about how to choose the supplement based on the probable cause of your insomnia.

If you feel tightness and stress, and stiffness around your body, consider taking Magnesium.

If you have recurrent repetitive, obsessive thoughts disrupting sleep, take Serotonin precursors like tryptophan or 5 HTP.

If you have irregular sleep hours or are traveling across different time zones, take melatonin.

If you move your leg a lot at night and feel restless - try iron and magnesium supplements.

If you have digestive problems, irregular bowel habits- take probiotics and fiber in your diet. It will aid in digestion and help sleep.

If you have frequent urination at night or prostate problems, try cranberry juice.

If you have severe anxiety, you can try the GABA supplements. For mild to moderate anxiety try the valerian root and essential herbs. If you have panic attacks, try inositol and B vitamins.

If you have sadness and depression impairing sleep- try the vitamin D and the omega 3 supplements. Major depression can be a life-threatening condition and always seek medical treatment.

If you have dizziness, balance problems, memory loss, fatigue, tingling – you may have Vitamin B 12 deficiency. Taking vitamin B supplements may be a good start.

In general, I tend to start all my patients on magnesium for sleep as the first step. Then depending on progress, and other symptoms, I add other supplements over time. I wait for a few months, if all fail- then consider less harmful sleep medications like Trazodone, Vistaril, Benadryl as the first step.

Another common approach of taking sleep supplements is in combination. Manufacturers combine lower doses of multiple supplements with the hope that the combination will create a synergy and help sleep efficiently. For some, combination of multiple products at lower doses are better tolerable, while some may need a few products at their maximal dosage.

Insomnitol is an example of a combination product made by the Designs for Health. Each bottle contains vegetarian capsules with the following ingredients list:

INSOMNITOL

Supplement Facts

Serving Size 2 capsules
Servings Per Container 30

Amount Per Serving		% Daily Value
Vitamin B-6 (as Pyridoxal-5-Phosphate)	10 mg	500%
Valerian (*Valeriana officinalis*)(root) [standardized to contain 0.8% valerenic acid]	400 mg	*
Passion Flower (*Passiflora incarnata*) (flower) [standardized to contain 3.5% flavonoids]	200 mg	*
Lemon Balm (*Melissa officinalis*)(leaves) [standardized to contain 3% rosmarinic acid]	200 mg	*
Chamomile (*Matricaria chamomilla)*(flower)	200 mg	*
gamma-Aminobutyric acid (as PharmaGABA™)	100 mg	*
L-Theanine	100 mg	
5-HTP (5-Hydroxytryptophan)	100 mg	*
Melatonin	3 mg	*

*Daily Value not established.

Other Ingredients: Cellulose (capsule), vegetable stearate, silicon dioxide.

In summary, supplements can be an essential tool in the treatment of insomnia, along with lifestyle changes, behavioral therapy, and medications. Be mindful that the Federal Drug Administration (FDA) does not regulate supplements as strictly it does for the prescription medications. Thus, doses and efficacy may vary. I have mentioned the standard treatment dosages in this article.

Always follow the manufacturer's recommendations as listed on the bottle under your doctor's guidance. As a rule, always start at the lowest dose and gradually go up, and never exceed the maximum recommended dose unless your physician says so. Sleep supplements work better if taken 1 hour before sleep.

Avoid driving or operating heavy machinery after taking them. There are many supplement brands on the market. The ones that I use for my patients are BrainMD, Jarrows, Designs for health, Pure Encapsulations, Thorne research, Mercola, and Zhou.

Be aware of the Side-effects of supplements. There is a common misconception that all supplements are natural and are free of side effects. This is false. Anything that can have a positive impact on the body can also have an adverse impact.

All supplements come with side effects; a cursory google search will bring out a list of them. The key is to use the right kind of supplement for the right person at the correct dosage. Many supplements can cross-react with other medications or supplements that you may be taking. Do your research to understand the risks and benefits. When in doubt, consult health professionals. Good luck and sleep deep!

CONCLUSION

Reading each book is like a personal journey. Congrats for finishing yours. I hope I have been able to convince you of the importance of sleep, and why it must be a priority in your life. Sleep is essential for survival, and some of the damages associated with long-term sleep deprivation are irreparable.

I also hope that the tools and remedies provided in the book will help to achieve your individual sleep goal. I will encourage you to keep reading, exploring and trying. There is a list of references and additional resources at the end. Whatever you read, always remember, you are the expert on your own body. Try different ways, see what works and what don't. In my clinical experience, I have realized that the human body is malleable, and it has broad potential. What works in the past, may not work in the future, and what failed in the past may work in the future with changing times and circumstances.

Lastly, we do not live in a perfect world. Things change, accidents do happen, everything always doesn't work according to plan. To survive, we have to improvise and adapt. I have sacrificed and lost sleep many times both willingly and unwillingly. I have forsaken sleep during exam-preparation, during medical studies, research, in caring for my patients, during night emergency, wife's pregnancy, newborn care, and other responsibilities. But I have also lost sleep for watching TV, movies, soap operas, and in other fun and frolic. I continue to work few nights a month in the care of patients.

Truth and knowledge empower us to set the right priorities. Let no one fool you in saying that lack of sleep has no implication. You may lose sleep because the only job available for your skill in your geography is the night shift. Or you are a caregiver for a family member and have to remain awake at night. Or you have a newborn or sick child, or you work in a 24x7 with changing shifts and hours. Whatever your situation is, I hope it is not long term. We may lose sleep, and if it is by choice, I hope it will be for a worthy cause. Everyone is entitled to refreshing, restful, peaceful sleep at night. I hope you get that too, and the book will only be a success if it can help you in so.

APPENDIX

FAMOUS SLEEP RESEARCHERS

Isaac Newton said in 1675, "If I have seen further it is by standing on the shoulders of Giants." This is also true for any field of scientific knowledge. Sleep-Research is new. The progress has been slow but steady. The following researchers have expanded and updated our understanding of the various aspects of Sleep. (Source: Wikipedia)

Hans Berger: German psychiatrist who invented Electroencephalography (EEG) in 1924. The EEG paved the path for all future sleep research. He suffered from depression and committed suicide in 1941.

Nathaniel Kleitman: (University of Chicago), a physiologist, opened the first sleep research lab in the USA. He is recognized as the father of modern sleep research and is the author of the seminal 1939 book- Sleep and Wakefulness.

Eugene Aserinksy: Discovered REM sleep in 1953 when he was doing his Ph.D. under Nathaniel Kleitman at the University of Chicago. He allegedly fell asleep while driving and died in a car accident.

William C Dement: (Stanford University)
Researched on sleep deprivation and the connection between REM sleep and dreams. He is also referred to as the father of American Sleep medicine.

Michel Jouvet: (University of Lyon, France)
Conducted several experiments on cats regarding muscle atonia (paralysis) during REM sleep. Identified REM as

independent paradoxical sleep.

Charles Czeisler (Harvard University), He made several contributions in his long carrier as a sleep researcher.

- 1990 – the Human circadian clock is highly light sensitive.
- 1995 – Blind people can still retain sleep rhythms if their eyes remain intact
- 1999 - Determined that the average circadian period in humans is 24.18 hours, not over 25 hours as previously thought
- 2002 – Invalidated findings that bright light behind the knees can impact human circadian rhythms.
- 2006 – Melatonin supplementation during the day can improve sleep quality at night and can be helpful to shift workers, people with jet-lag as well as people with circadian rhythm sleep disorders.
- 2006 - Task performance while chronically sleep deprived suffers severely
- 2013 – Sleep deprivation causes changes in normal gene expression and can negatively impact health.

David F. Dinges: (University of Pennsylvania School of Medicine)

Dinges' work has contributed to our knowledge of the effects of sleep disorders, the recovery potential of naps, the nature of sleep inertia and the impact of cumulative sleep debt.

Mark R. Rosekind: Internationally-recognized expert in fatigue management.

John Allan Hobson: (Harvard Medical School)
An American psychiatrist and dream researcher, well-known for his research on different aspects and meaning of dreams.

Robert Stickgold: (Harvard Medical School)

A preeminent sleep researcher, dedicated his life to understanding the relationship between sleep, learning, dreaming and memory consolidation.

SLEEP QUOTATIONS

"It is a common experience that a problem difficult at night is resolved in the morning after the committee of sleep has worked on it." - *John Steinbeck*

"Laugh and the world laughs with you; snore, and you sleep alone!" - *Anthony Burgess*

"A well-spent day brings happy sleep." - *Leonardo da Vinci*

"Sleep that knits up the ravelled sleave of care;
The death of each day's life, sore labour's bath;
Balm of hurt minds, great nature's second course;
Chief nourisher in life's feast."
- *William Shakespeare, Macbeth*

"Sleep is the interest we have to pay on the capital which is called in at death; and the higher the rate of interest and the more regularly it is paid, the further the date of redemption is postponed." - *Arthur Schopenhauer*

"Your life is a reflection of how you sleep, and how you sleep is a reflection of your life." - *Dr. Rafael Pelayo*

"Think in the morning. Act in the noon. Eat in the evening. Sleep in the night." *William Blake*

To achieve the impossible dream, try going to sleep." *Joan Klempner*

And if tonight my soul may find her peace in sleep, and sink in good oblivion, and in the morning wake like a new opened flower then I have been dipped again in God, and new created."

D.H. Lawrence

"Death, so called, is a thing which makes men weep: And yet a third of Life is passed in sleep." *Lord Byron*

"For sleep, one needs endless depths of blackness to sink into; daylight is too shallow, it will not cover one." Anne Morrow Lindbergh

Early to bed and early to rise makes a man healthy, wealthy, and wise. Fatigue is the best pillow" *Benjamin Franklin.*

"Sleep is the best meditation"- *Dalai Lama.*

LINKS TO MINDFULNESS COURSES:

The Art of Living Foundation

http://www.artofliving.org/us-en

Transcendental Meditation

https://www.tm.org/enlightenment

Self-Realization Fellowship

https://www.yogananda-srf.org/

The Heartfulness

Way https://theheartfulnessway.com/

GOOD BOOKS ON SLEEP

At Day's Close: Night in Times by A. Roger Ekirch

Dreaming: An Introduction to the Science of Sleep by John Hobson

John Durant – The Paleo Manifesto: Ancient Wisdom for Lifelong Health by John Durant

Eat Move Sleep by Tom Rath

The Promise of Sleep by William C. Dement

The End of Night by Paul Bogard

Light Out- Sleep, Sugar, and Survival by TS Wiley & Bent Formby

Say Good Night to Insomnia by Gregg D. Jacobs

The Happiest Baby Guide to Great Sleep by Harvey Karp

The Secret World of Sleep by Penelope A. Lewis

The Secret Life of Sleep by Kat Duff

Sleep Interrupted by Steven Y. Park, M.D

Secrets of Sleep Science: From Dreams to Disorders, Great Courses Lecture Series by Professor H. Craig Heller

GOOD BOOKS ON NATURAL HEALTH

Stress Rescue by Panch Paul & Bob Kamath

The End of Alzheimer's: The First Program to Prevent and Reverse Cognitive Decline by Dale Bredesen

Finally Focused: The Breakthrough Natural Treatment Plan for ADHD by Greenblatt, James

Change Your Brain, Change Your Life: by Daniel G. Amen M.D

The Power of Habit: Why We Do What We Do in Life and Business Paperback
by Charles Duhigg

Mosby's Handbook of Herbs & Natural Supplements 4th Edition by Linda Skidmore-Roth RN MSN NP

Deep Work: Rules for Focused Success in a Distracted World Hardcover by Cal Newport

Nutrition and Physical Degeneration by Weston Price

The Blue Zones: Lessons for Living Longer from the People Who've Lived the Longest by Dan Buettner

REFERENCES

What is Sleep?

http://www.helpguide.org/articles/sleep/how-much-sleep-do-you-need.htm

http://www.ninds.nih.gov/disorders/brain_basics/understanding_sleep.htm#dreaming

http://www.aasmnet.org/jcsm/Articles/030203.pdf

http://medical-dictionary.thefreedictionary.com/sleep

http://www.ncbi.nlm.nih.gov/pubmed/10643753

Sleep Regulation & Insomnia

http://www.ncbi.nlm.nih.gov/pmc/articles/PMC1978319/

"Sleep Wake Disorders." Diagnostic and statistical manual of mental disorders: DSM-5. 5th ed. Washington, D.C.: American Psychiatric Association, 2013.

Phases of Sleep

Thomas A. Wehr: In short photoperiods, human sleep is biphasic

http://onlinelibrary.wiley.com/doi/10.1111/j.1365-2869.1992.tb00019.x/pdf

At Day's Close: Night in Times by A. Roger Ekirch

SLEEP HEALING IN ANCIENT TIMES

Wilcox, Robert A; Whitham, Emma M (15 April 2003). "The symbol of modern medicine: why one snake is more than two." Annals of Internal Medicine **138**: 673–7.

doi:10.7326/0003-4819-138-8-200304150-00016. PMID 12693891.

Sigerist. Chapter 3, Religious medicine: Asclepius and his cult, p. 63ff.

Dawson, Warren R. (1929). Magician and Leech: A Study in the Beginnings of Medicine with Special Reference to Ancient Egypt. London: Methuen.

Garry, T. Gerald (1931). Egypt: The Home of the Occult Sciences, with Special Reference to Imhotep, the Mysterious Wise Man and Egyptian God of Medicine. London: John Bale, Sons and Danielsson.

Dreams

http://dreamtraining.blogspot.se/2010/12/inventions-that-came-in-dreams-largest.html

http://www.world-of-lucid-dreaming.com/why-do-we-dream.html

http://www.lisashea.com/lisabase/dreams/inspirations/index.html

http://writetodone.com/use-your-dreams-to-be-endlessly-creative/

http://jamesclear.com/markus-zusak

http://www.world-of-lucid-dreaming.com/10-dreams-that-changed-the-course-of-human-history.html

http://www.theepochtimes.com/n3/1388633-4-more-scientific-discoveries-made-in-dreams/

http://www.brilliantdreams.com/product/famous-dreams.htm

http://mentalfloss.com/article/12763/11-creative-breakthroughs-people-had-their-sleep

http://www.famousscientists.org/7-great-examples-of-scientific-discoveries-made-in-dreams/

Sleep Deprivation & Driving

https://www.cdc.gov/features/dsdrowsydriving/index.html

http://timesofindia.indiatimes.com/entertainment/hindi/bollywood/news/How-does-Akshay-Kumar-manage-to-do-so-many-films-in-a-year/articleshow/45046075.cms

Sleep & Lifespan & Blue Zone

https://www.bluezones.com/about-blue-zones/

https://www.bluezones.com/2013/09/9-blue-zones-lessons-for-slowing-down/

Danish twin studies:

http://www.ncbi.nlm.nih.gov/pubmed/8786073/

Nap Benefits

http://www.ncbi.nlm.nih.gov/pubmed/12819785

http://www.huffingtonpost.com/2014/05/06/famous-people-who-nap_n_5248739.html

http://sleepfoundation.org/sleep-topics/sleep-drive-and-your-body-clock

http://www.misd.net/secondaryliteracy/PracticeAssessment/Grade7/Grade_7_PT_Napping_Explanatory_478940_7.pdf

http://www.jetlog.com/fileadmin/downloads/AS_StratNapsOpsSet.pdf

http://science.nasa.gov/science-news/science-at-nasa/2005/03jun_naps/

http://www.nimh.nih.gov/news/science-news/2008/caffeine-no-substitute-for-a-nap-to-enhance-memory.shtml
http://www.webmd.com/sleep-disorders/features/america-its-time-for-your-nap?page=2

http://sleepfoundation.org/sleep-topics/napping

http://science.nasa.gov/science-news/science-at-nasa/2001/ast04sep_1/

Brooks, A; Lack, L. (2006). "A brief afternoon nap following nocturnal sleep restriction: which nap duration is most recuperative?". Sleep (29). p. 831-840. Retrieved 2015-04-18.

Jump up ^ "The effects of a 20-min nap before post-lunch dip". 1998-04-01. Retrieved 2008-06-12.

http://www.ncbi.nlm.nih.gov/pubmed/17296887

http://www.nytimes.com/2007/02/01/fashion/01skin.html?pagewanted=all&_r=0

http://news.bbc.co.uk/2/hi/uk_news/magazine/7114661.stm

http://www.theguardian.com/world/2014/aug/18/japanese-firms-encourage-workers-sleep-on-job.

http://www.bbc.com/news/blogs-news-from-elsewhere-28364606

Sleep & Alarm time & Waking

http://www.mcall.com/news/nationworld/mc-nws-study-later-school-start-times-20170901-story.html

http://pediatrics.aappublications.org/content/early/2014/08/19/peds.2014-1697

What is Circadian Rhythm?

https://sleepfoundation.org/sleep-topics/sleep-drive-and-your-body-clock

http://symposium.cshlp.org/content/72/579.full.pdf

The American Psychiatric Publishing Textbook of Psychiatry, Sleep Wake disorders, Page 608

24.2-Hour Sleep Cycle

http://www.ncbi.nlm.nih.gov/pubmed/18419318

https://justgetflux.com/

Food for Sleep

https://sleepfoundation.org/sleep-topics/food-and-drink-promote-good-nights-sleep

Sleep Habits

Onen SH, Onen F, Bailly D, Parquet P. Prevention and treatment of sleep disorders through regulation of sleeping habits. Presse Med.1994; Mar 12; 23(10): 485-9.

National Sleep Foundation: The Sleep Environment

http://www.sleepfoundation.org/article/how-sleep-works/the-sleep-environment

Sleep Environment

Onen SH, Onen F, Bailly D, Parquet P. Prevention and treatment of sleep disorders through regulation of sleeping habits. Presse Med.1994; Mar 12; 23(10): 485-9.

National Sleep Foundation: The Sleep Environment

http://www.sleepfoundation.org/article/how-sleep-works/the-sleep-environment

http://www.huffingtonpost.com/dr-christopher-winter/best-temperature-for-sleep_b_3705049.html

http://www.webmd.com/sleep-disorders/features/cant-sleep-adjust-the-temperature?page=2

(http://healthland.time.com/2011/06/17/tip-for-insomniacs-cool-your-head-to-fall-asleep/)

Sleep Apnea Diagnosis & Treatment

The Promise of Sleep by William C Dement, MD,

https://www.ncbi.nlm.nih.gov/pubmed/24061345

https://www.ncbi.nlm.nih.gov/pubmed/16855960

https://www.ncbi.nlm.nih.gov/pubmed/24077936

https://www.ncbi.nlm.nih.gov/pubmed/22549673

Sleep Apnea Prevention

Kushida, C., B. Efron, C. Guilleminault. A Predictive Morphometric Model for the Obstructive Sleep Apnea Syndrome. Ann Intern Med 1997; 127(8):581-7. http://www.brianpalmerdds.com/pdf/master_2_27_06.pdf.

breastfeeding Abstracts, February 1999. Volume 18, Number 3, Pages 19-20, Author: Brian Palmer, D.D.S., Kansas City, Missouri

http://www.brianpalmerdds.com/bfing_import.htm

http://www.amazon.com/The-Land-Naked-People-Encounters/dp/B000C4SN1C

(http://articles.mercola.com/sites/articles/archive/2011/05/21/dr-arthur-strauss-on-sleep-apnea.aspx)

http://www.ncbi.nlm.nih.gov/pmc/articles/PMC4216726

http://doctorstevenpark.com/whats-the-best-sleep-position

Sleep for Babies

Here is the link to the website site of Professor James J. McKenna who is recognized as the world's leading authority on mother-infant co-sleeping in relationship to breastfeeding and SIDS:

http://cosleeping.nd.edu/safe-co-sleeping-guidelines/

Those who are interested to know about the co-sleeping concerns and current debates can refer to the blog of Dr. Sears who is the expert on attachment parenting: https://www.askdrsears.com/news/latest-news/dr-sears-addresses-recent-co-sleeping-concerns

https://cosleeping.nd.edu/safe-co-sleeping-guidelines/

Sleep Supplements

Many of the supplement guidelines are taken from Dr. James Greenblatt's who is an expert on Integrative Psychiatry. For more details, refer to his books-

Breakthrough Depression Solution: Mastering Your Mood with Nutrition, Diet & Supplementation

Finally Focused: The Breakthrough Natural Treatment Plan for ADHD

# ACKNOWLEDGEMENT

I started working on this book in 2016. It has been a long process with many bumps and delays. Many have helped me in this process and encouraged me to continue. I will like to thank my mentors Dr. Adolf Casal, Dr. Roy Sanders, Dr. Todd Antin, Dr. Arden Dingle, Dr. Daniel Rapport, Dr. Barry Hensel for showing faith in me. Also, thanks to doctors Akshay Lokhande, Abhimanyu Ghose, Ankush Moza, DJ Singh, Anjali Nayak, Puneet Singla, Sajaad Sarwar, Ajay Singh, Ahmed Janjua, and Alina Rais, and John Wryobeck.

I am also grateful to Dr. Daniel Amen, Dr. Rob Johnson, Dr. Muneer Ali, Dr. Ben Nelson, Dr. Jay Faber, and Dr. James Greenblatt for their guidance on the integrative approach to brain health. Also, thanks to Dr. Iqbal Dhanani, Dr. Sailesh Patel, Dr. Shahzad Hashmi, Dr. Ashraff Attala, Dr. Asaf Aleem, and Dr. Joe Bona. Also, thanks to Dr. Sumit Ranjan, and Dr. Suprateek Kundu, Praveen Khemka, Sushobhan Gupta, and Dr. Bhupesh Barman.

Lastly, all I have done and accomplished in life is because of my family support. My father Pratul Paul and mother Kshama Paul has made many sacrifices to make me a doctor and send to the US. My wife Sagnika, and sister Chandramallika for always being there. And to my grandfather HL Kundu for his teachings and inspiration.

Lastly, to all the wonderful people who gave me the opportunity to treat them and taught me in the process.

ABOUT THE AUTHOR

Dr. Panchajanya Paul is a double Board Certified – Child, Adolescent, and Adult Psychiatrist. He is a diplomat of the American Board of Integrative and Holistic Medicine (ABIHM). He is a diplomate of the American Board of Psychiatry and Neurology (ABPN). He completed his general psychiatry training at the University of Toledo Medical Center in Ohio in 2011. He completed his child & adolescent psychiatry fellowship training at the EMORY University in 2013. He received training in holistic medicine from the Scripps Center for Integrative Medicine in San Diego in 2014. He was also trained by Dr. Daniel Amen in the use of SPECT scan, QEEG, and supplements at the Amen Clinics in 2017.

Dr. Paul grew up in India and finished his medical training at the Manipal University which is ranked among the top ten medical school in India. He graduated with honors and the distinction of being among the top 5 of his class. He treats the whole person and provides holistic psychiatric care. He incorporates medications, supplements, therapy, genomics, sleep, diet, exercise and mindfulness in his treatment plan. He enjoys working with all age groups- individually, as well as couples and families.

Dr. Paul specializes in the use complementary and alternative medicine like natural herbs and supplements in treating anxiety, depression, and ADHD. He has helped many patients get better using natural and complimentary methods while using minimal or no medications.

Dr. Paul is passionate about teaching and writing. He holds adjunct faculty positions at Emory University School of Medicine; University of Georgia & Georgia Regents University; and University of Central Florida School of Medicine. He is a freelance writer and runs health columns for three local news magazines in Atlanta. In the past, he had served as a medical director of Harbor Pines, one of the largest Crisis stabilization unit in Florida. He has also worked as a staff psychiatrist at the Amen Clinics, Atlanta, and the Atlanta Center of Eating Disorders.

Sleep Coaching is the second book by Dr. Panchajanya Paul. His first book is called 'Stress Rescue', coauthored with Dr. Bob Kamath, published in July 2018. Dr. Paul currently does private practice in Atlanta, Georgia. For all his contributions to the field of psychiatry, Dr. Paul was made a Fellow of the American Psychiatric Association (FAPA) in 2016.

Made in the USA
Columbia, SC
11 November 2021

48791116R00143